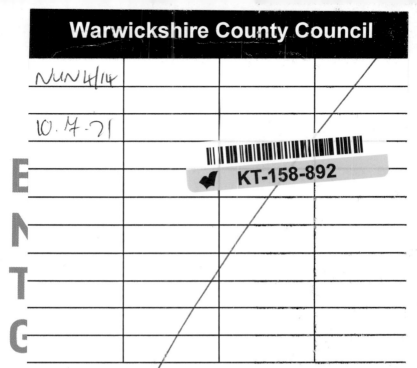

PEARSON

At Pearson, we believe in learning – all kinds of learning for all kinds of people. Whether it's at home, in the classroom or in the workplace, learning is the key to improving our life chances.

That's why we're working with leading authors to bring you the latest thinking and best practices, so you can get better at the things that are important to you. You can learn on the page or on the move, and with content that's always crafted to help you understand quickly and apply what you've learned.

If you want to upgrade your personal skills or accelerate your career, become a more effective leader or more powerful communicator, discover new opportunities or simply find more inspiration, we can help you make progress in your work and life.

Pearson is the world's leading learning company. Our portfolio includes the Financial Times and our education business, Pearson International.

Every day our work helps learning flourish, and wherever learning flourishes, so do people.

To learn more, please visit us at www.pearson.com/uk

Business Networking – The Survival Guide

How to make networking less about stress and more about success

WILL KINTISH

Harlow, England • London • New York • Boston • San Francisco • Toronto • Sydney
Auckland • Singapore • Hong Kong • Tokyo • Seoul • Taipei • New Delhi
Cape Town • São Paulo • Mexico City • Madrid • Amsterdam • Munich • Paris • Milan

PEARSON EDUCATION LIMITED
Edinburgh Gate
Harlow CM20 2JE
United Kingdom
Tel: +44 (0)1279 623623
Web: www.pearson.com/uk

First published 2014 (print and electronic)

Pearson Education is not responsible for the content of third-party internet sites.

ISBN: 978-1-292-00937-7 (print)
       978-1-292-00938-4 (PDF)
       978-1-292-00939-1 (ePub)
       978-1-292-00940-7 (eText)

British Library Cataloguing-in-Publication Data
A catalogue record for the print edition is available from the British Library

Library of Congress Cataloging-in-Publication Data
Kintish, Will.
  Business networking, the survival guide : how to make networking less about stress and more about success / Will Kintish.
     pages cm
Includes index.
ISBN 978-1-292-00937-7
1. Business networks. I. Title.
HD69.S8K536 2014
650.1'3--dc23
                              2014001196

The publisher is grateful to Alan Stevens for permission to reproduce the quote on page 15.

10 9 8 7 6 5 4 3 2 1
18 17 16 15 14

Cover design by Dan Mogford
Cartoons drawn by Peter Entwistle

Print edition typeset in 9.5/13pt ITC Giovanni Std by 30
Print edition printed and bound in Great Britain by Henry Ling Ltd, at the Dorset Press, Dorchester, Dorset

NOTE THAT ANY PAGE CROSS REFERENCES REFER TO THE PRINT EDITION

Contents

About the author

Will Kintish FCA FPSA qualified as a chartered accountant in 1971 and was in general practice for the next 30 years.

At the start of the twenty-first century he changed his career and since then has shown thousands in the academic, professional, financial and third-sector communities how to become more effective and confident networkers. Networking is fundamental to success, yet so many people fear it. Will shows you how to overcome all your fears and concerns when working the room, how to spot potential opportunities and how to follow up in a professional manner.

Since 2009 he has become a leading exponent and advisor on the professional social networking site LinkedIn, showing thousands of delegates how to use it as a vital career and business development tool in combination with face-to-face networking.

He is a Fellow of the Professional Speaking Association, the highest accolade available in the speaking profession. Whether running workshops, speaking online 'to the computer' or giving keynote speeches, he communicates with passion, enthusiasm and lots of humour.

As he will tell you, these days it's his birthday every day: 'Well, after 30 years in the wrong job, it would be your birthday every day too!'

Acknowledgements

It is over 40 years since I left school. This seems an appropriate moment to reflect on some of the people and organisations who have been a major, positive influence on my life. To those people I am deeply indebted.

I'm sure there are lots more. Thank you also to those people who are not listed here.

Johnny Apples	My crazy marketing consultant
Baker Tilly	For showing me the way out of accountancy
Chris Barrow	For introducing me to business coaching
Nita Bookin	My 11+ English tutor
Dale Carnegie	My original and constant inspiration
Arnold Clarke	My first boss, who gave me an opportunity to show what I was capable of
Friends and family	Because they're friends and family
Phil Greene	My good friend
Robert Grindrod	A great influencer and a good friend
John Hansford	Headmaster, Bury Grammar School
Kintish children – Joanne, Michael, Antony, Jonathan, Susannah and Laura	For putting up with my constant enthusiasm and passion about networking

ACKNOWLEDGEMENTS

Trudie Kintish	My wife, inspiration and parachute!
Gareth Lewis	The man who changed my life
Natalie Lewis	My first work colleague at Kintish
Manchester Business Breakfast Club	My weekly networking colleagues, who entertain, encourage and recommend business members
Ivan Misner	The founder of BNI (Business Network International)
Professional Speaking Association fellow members	Inspiring, helpful and caring colleagues, who are ready to support – constantly
Referrers, and introducers of new work	My free 'sales force'
Peter Thomson	My price consultant and constant mentor
Sue Tonks	My original presentation skills coach and senior associate

Foreword

Networking is one of the most important techniques for people who want to build their business. No matter what country or what culture we come from, we all speak the language of referrals. Yet we are not teaching the next generation of business professionals anything about building their business through networking or word-of-mouth marketing! Virtually no academic books on business or marketing focus on this area. Consequently, scores of young people are graduating with college degrees in business and marketing but have not one iota of training in an area that almost all business practitioners agree is one of the most critical to the success of any enterprise.

Structured networking programmes can make the difference between success and failure. A systematic networking effort is also personally empowering; it's one of the few things that you, or someone who works for you, can do that directly affects success.

Why wait for people to walk through your door? Why sit idly, hoping that your existing clients or customers will refer you to others? With a structured networking programme, you don't have to wait for the results of your last PR campaign to kick in. Networking gives you control and allows you to take ownership of the development of your business. Such a programme has worked for millions of people in all types of businesses – and will work for you as well.

Will Kintish's excellent book will help anyone to become a better networker. I have worked with tens of thousands of business professionals, helping them to develop successful networking programmes, and I can categorically state that if you follow the ideas outlined in this book, you will develop your networking expertise and enhance your abilities to build a word-of-mouth based business through networking. *Business Networking* is all about building your business by developing relationships and working with your contacts. I am sure that if you follow Will's advice you will greatly enhance your chances of success through networking.

Ivan R. Misner
Founder of BNI (Business Network International) and bestselling
author of *Masters of Networking*

How this book works

Who am I?

Will: *Allow me to introduce myself. My name is Will and my role in life is to help you and other professionals, academics and business owners become more confident and effective networkers. If you listen to my tips, techniques and ideas, I promise that networking will become a lot easier, more enjoyable, and, more importantly, you'll leave every event you attend with something useful.*

I'm an authority on networking and have presented to and trained 70,000+ business, professional and academic people to be more effective and confident networkers. I've heard all the worries, fear and excuses before, so don't worry – you're in safe hands.

I know what works, what you should do and how to make networking events more enjoyable and productive for you. In fact, I've developed an eight-step networking pipeline that (when you follow it) will increase your number of business connections and possible opportunities for you.

Here it is. You'll learn more about each stage as we go through the book.

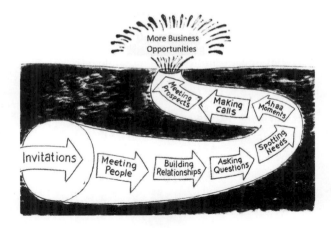

This has been developed from years of experience and, if followed, it will produce the results you're looking for.

I've written this book to help you from start to finish – we begin from the moment the invitation arrives, to what to do at the event, through to following up afterwards and how to create real opportunities and keep those new connections.

You'll meet Brian, who's a bit like you. He has an event to go to, but he doesn't like networking. We'll follow him step by step on his journey to the networking event, and beyond.

Brian: *Hello, I'm Brian. There'll be more from me later on.*

etworking important?

rking is *not* about selling you or your company.
rking is about spotting possible opportunities – do they
problem you can help with, or would working together
ething help both of you?

rking builds relationships. People prefer to do busi-
ith people they like and trust, so spending time on
g a relationship could deliver results in the future.

rking is expected. Even if your role isn't explicitly
g in new business or to market the company, you are
ly expected, as most people are, to meet new people
derstand the market place as part of your role.

king is good for you. You'll learn more about the
s landscape, and understand your industry better and
our prospects.

king can further your career. The vast majority of
never advertised but are filled by recommendations.
efinitely a case of who you know …

king is a virtuous circle. If done right, meeting more
leads to more business and career opportunities,
ads to meeting more people and more business, and

rking is about spotting
opportunities –would
together on something
h of you?"

d be reading this book?

d expect me to say 'everyone', but, no, let's be a little
d.

looking for your first or next job, the very best way
is through meeting the right people. If you don't

want to take your chance through bureaux and responding to adverts, this book is for you.

- If you are in the professional and financial worlds, you might want to move up the success ladder faster than others. When you create new business opportunities of your own, rather than waiting for others to contact you or more senior people to throw opportunities at you, you will be quickly noticed. If you want to become that 'rainmaker', this book is for you.

- If you are in academia and need to build relationships with business to develop alliances and partnerships, this book is for you.

- If you are in business and feel the business is not growing as you would like it because to date you have been too reactive, this book is for you.

- If you are young (20–30ish!) you will be in a generation that has become immersed in social media. This environment is important, but a strong word of advice: there is no substitute for having outstanding interpersonal communication skills. Whether you are looking for a new role or you are in business development you will be doing yourself a disservice by not selling yourself in the first instance to the prospective employer or customer. Your academic degrees and professional credentials alone are no longer enough to achieve your full potential. If you struggle with groups of people in any circumstances, this book is for you.

"If you are looking for your first or next job, the best way to find it is through meeting the right people."

The international angle

The advice I am about to share with you is relevant to the UK and most English-speaking communities, but there will be a number of customs and behaviours I mention that will be total 'no no's' in other countries. Across the world, different cultures will have numerous nuances in their accepted behaviours that would make it irresponsible to suggest a uniform approach to understanding any country's social/business culture or etiquette. We must also take into account the personal cultures of individuals, whether they be religious, regional, gender, corporate or otherwise.

Here are some key pointers to watch for:

- Note the ceremony of business cards in Japan and other Asian countries.
- Be careful of handshakes with the opposite sex in certain countries and religions.
- The casual use of the first name in the UK and US generally will not go down well in others countries.
- Eye contact in certain parts of the world will not be acceptable.
- Although here in the UK we prefer to avoid talking about religion and politics, in other countries they love these topics.
- Arriving too early or late for a meeting or event are two other variables which need consideration depending on where in the world you are.
- Be sensitive with your body language: misunderstandings over gestures can cause embarrassment and can lead to business complications.

I could write a whole book on these cultural differences. Suffice it to say here that if you attend business events in other countries, remember to do your homework!

"If you attend business events in other countries, remember to do your homework!"

PS

At the end of each chapter I will share three key points I think are worth learning and using.

1. Networking is a process; follow it and you will become a top-class networker.

2. Whether you are in a job or looking for a job, you need to become proficient at networking to fulfil your true potential.

3. When you do business outside your own country, make sure you know exactly what the business customs are.

Part

1

Before the event

Chapter

1

The invitation

The networking life of Brian

Brian's office 9:15 a.m. Four weeks before the event. Brian is sorting out his post.

> **B:** *Right, what have we here? Letters from clients, junk mail, ah, what's this – an invitation to a networking event? I hate those events … waste of time … I'm going to bin it. Not for me, thank you.*

If you've ever been invited to an event through work and not wanted to go, you're not alone. Many of us have felt uncomfortable about going to networking events. But don't worry, it's entirely natural. Listed below are some of the common reasons why people don't like to attend networking events.

"If you've ever been invited to an event and not wanted to go, you're not alone."

Why don't you want to go?

- I don't like it – I feel uncomfortable.
- I probably won't know anyone there.
- My hosts hardly recommend any work to us, so what's the point?
- They're bound to invite 150+ people and I'll feel like a fish out of water.
- I can't remember the last time I went and came back thinking it was time well spent.

All these reasons are very common, but there are in fact some very good reasons why you should go.

Why should you go?

- **Get in the driving seat**. It's a chance for you to raise your own and your organisation's profile rather than waiting for people to find you.
- **It's a chance for you to develop your business**. Don't rely on others to keep sending referrals and making introductions for you. When you get involved, you'll see a real uplift in activity for your business.
- **You never know who you might meet**. There's every chance you'll meet a useful contact or a prospective client.
- **Raise your personal profile externally**. You'll be noticed by people outside your firm in and out of your business sector. It's a great opportunity to broaden your horizons.

- **Raise your profile internally.** Your boss and colleagues will be delighted you're going to networking events. Surveys show that when you do a great job and you're visible, your chances of promotion are much greater.

- **You may learn something.** Meeting new people in your own or other professions or your local area might reveal some interesting opportunities for you or your business.

- **You might actually have a good time.** Everyone attending a networking event wants to have a good time so you're all in the same boat.

The 'ahaa' moment

But most importantly, do you *really* know why you should go networking? If sometimes you're not quite sure ... read on.

Of course the simple answer is 'to get more business' or 'find that dream job'. This is correct, but sometimes it's easier said than done. A major part of the process is spotting the 'ahaa' moment. The 'ahaa' moment is when you ask pertinent and searching questions and the other person says something that makes your heart pound a little faster and you think 'Ahaa, this could be a potential business or career opportunity'.

> **"The 'ahaa' moment is when you ask pertinent questions and the other person says something that makes your heart pound a little faster."**

What does an 'ahaa' sound like?

- Yes, our present advisors are brilliant but ...
- We have a problem with ...
- We're struggling with ...
- They're OK, but ...
- They don't look after us like they used to.

- They're fine but our present contact is leaving/retiring.
- They're rubbish.
- We don't feel we're getting the right advice.
- We didn't know that.
- We need to learn more about that.
- We're thinking of ...
- Oh no, not another accountant/lawyer.
- That's interesting, tell me more ...
- We've never heard of that.
- We don't understand what we get for our money.
- We rarely hear from them.
- They're not very proactive.
- They never told us that.
- We pay far too much.
- Our biggest issue is ...
- I might be interested in that.
- We're looking for someone like you.
- Someone is leaving.

Action and non-action

If you think you have met a person/business you wish to work with and you or your colleagues have the appropriate knowledge, expertise and experience to help, then it's time to start the follow-up process. But it's time *not to sell*.

When you hear one of the above phrases, just keep asking more gentle questions. Don't compare your business to their existing providers and of course don't even suggest criticism. Keep the whole focus on them and their issues, then ask the question ... the most important question in the whole conversation: 'You know you said ... [the 'ahaa' comment] ... well, how do you feel/ would you mind if I call you in the next day or so, so that I can hear more about your company/the issue and if you think it's relevant then perhaps we could meet up to discuss it further?'

Back to that invitation

Receiving an invitation is the first part of the networking pipeline.

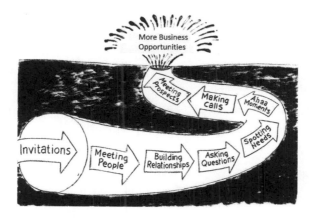

If you don't act on that invitation, you can't follow the pipeline through and realise those opportunities that are waiting for you.

Networking is a skill, and unless you know what to do and how to do it well, you're bound to find networking events difficult and unsettling. But it doesn't have to be that way, and this book will show you tried and tested rules to make any networking event more enjoyable and more worthwhile for you.

"Networking is a skill, and unless you know what to do, you're bound to find networking events difficult."

W: *That event you've been invited to. Look – the invitation you're holding. Why don't you give it a go? Stick with me for this one event and let's see what happens. You might be surprised …*

B: *OK, Will. I'll go to this event, but I just know it's going to be a waste of time. Where's that invitation …?*

W: *Good. Stay with me, Brian. I'll give you all the support you need.*

PS

1. Never ignore an invitation. Even if you can't go, you should always respond politely. Not only does it put you and your company in a good light, it also means they'll consider you for other future events.

2. If you can't go, suggest a colleague goes in your place. They might be able to go, and it means your organisation will still be represented.

3. Always look for something positive to take home from the event – it's called the 'ahaa' moment!

Chapter

2

Your LinkedIn profile (and how it fits into networking)

This is who I am

The only time we tend to think about and write down our present and past work experiences and our general interests is when we decide to change our job or career. It's called a CV or résumé. But why not use LinkedIn to post this information for the entire world to see at any time?

It doesn't matter whether your prospective contacts are on LinkedIn or not, as when you organise your settings correctly anyone can see your profile.

> **W:** *Brian, I know it's bringing a whole new concept to networking, but you need to start to embrace social networking (sometimes it's called social media). This to ensure you're a top-class networker both face-to-face and online in today's hi-tech world. It will never replace 'the real thing', but when you work the two in harness it will be a great cocktail for business opportunities.*

Building relationships

Networking is all about building relationships and every relationship we have ever built is based on three key stages: know; like; trust. We can't very easily get to like and trust people online, but we can get to know them. That is where an attractive and interesting profile comes in.

"Every relationship we have ever built is based on three key stages: know; like; trust."

Today we all need to be visible online; in fact, a strategy for success is visibility. Social networking and the internet is here to stay and if you want to 'keep up' you really do need to tell the world who you are, what you do and what area of expertise you have. You may be concerned about your privacy and if so it is unlikely you are on Facebook. (Facebook generally is for fun and social activity, whereas LinkedIn is a showcase for you in a professional setting.) But why not use LinkedIn to promote yourself in today's ever competitive and challenging marketing place? You don't need to brag or boast, just tell those who may be interested who you are and how you may be able to add value to their business.

What goes on your profile?

It is very important that from the start you see your LinkedIn profile as a document about who you are as a person, not just facts about you as a partner, manager, researcher, etc. It should be a pen-picture that gives the reader a good initial view as to what sort of a person you are. Just like in face-to-face networking, the start of a relationship is all about first impressions, so ensure your profile is complete, has no spelling or grammatical errors and is as up to date as possible.

As you start to fill in your profile, LinkedIn tells you how comprehensive it is. You will be guided to the sections you need to complete it fully.

A comprehensive LinkedIn profile should include:

- your industry and location
- an up-to-date current position (with a description)
- two past positions
- your education

- your skills (minimum of three)
- a profile photo
- at least 50 connections.

Your picture

This paragraph has been taken from my friend Alan Stevens' website (**www.mediacoach.co.uk**) and as it was so perfect I have reproduced it here:

> It's often said (probably because it's true) that social networking is about personal relationships. All social networking sites give you the opportunity to upload a picture to your profile, so I find it remarkable that many people don't bother. Personally, I rarely follow anyone on Twitter who doesn't have a photo. It's about honesty (so make sure it's a picture of you too).

> Some people take the opportunity to upload a picture of their family pet, their children, or a snap of themselves on their wedding day. That's fine if you never expect to do business with anyone. But if you want to make a good impression, have a nice, smiley head and shoulders picture and not the one in the Metallica T-shirt (unless you're a tattoo artist).

Key words

Your public profile, the one anyone searching your name sees, is indexed by Google, Yahoo! etc. The more complete your profile, the higher up the rankings you get, so ensure your main areas of expertise are mentioned on your profile.

The line below your name is critical if you want people to find out what you do, not just what you are. Rather than putting 'Partner at Company ABC' it is better to put 'Working hard at reducing your tax bill' or 'Advising you on your business strategy in the X area'.

Here is my own sales pitch … it's very short:

> I show people how to enhance their face-to-face networking skills and how to profit from the use of LinkedIn. My advice is for anyone who attends business events in any capacity and who needs to get real value when using LinkedIn.

When you view my LinkedIn profile you see the phrases 'Business networking' and 'LinkedIn trainer/Training' featuring a number of times. This means when people look for those skills my profile ranks very high against others offering the same services.

Your summary

After your name, photo, present and past jobs, and education headlines comes the section headed 'Summary'. This is where you tell people who you are as a person. Let them understand your personality, your passions, your values. If possible keep it light-hearted (if you're that sort of person). My summary paragraph starts with:

> Thank you for stopping by. I think I am one of the very lucky guys on this planet. I just love what I do, so much so that some people will call me a workaholic. Maybe I am but ... Confucius said many years ago, 'Give someone a job they love and they will never have to work a day in their life'. The tangible rewards of the job are fine, but if I was a multi-millionaire I would do what I do for nothing. I aim to be a kind and giving person. Do I always achieve this? Only those I am in contact with can tell you this.

Within the summary section there is a space for specialities; include here all your knowledge expertise and what your experience is.

Top tips

- There are sections for you to enter details of your previous job roles. Don't just say you worked at the firm for six years. If you are proud of your achievements there, say so. Your profile is a modest-free zone ... without showing off.
- You have three opportunities to promote your website(s) and various pages on them. LinkedIn gives you default phrases like 'My company' 'My blog' 'My website'. Again using the settings buttons you can change these to be more personal and informative.

- There are sections for projects you have been involved in, books and articles you have written, qualifications, degrees and awards you have achieved. You have worked hard for all these, no doubt, so be proud and mention them.

Are you an 'all-rounded' person?

The beauty of LinkedIn is that you decide exactly what you want others to know about you. If you just show details of your work life people may get an impression of you that is not what you'd like.

> "The beauty of LinkedIn is that you decide exactly what you want others to know about you."

Facebook users seem to show all sorts of photographs, some of which could be there to hang them in the future, and tell their friends and/or everyone everything about their personal lives. I suggest on LinkedIn you at least headline your personal interests outside work, what organisations you belong to and give more detail about your education. This is all based around you as a professional and shows what sort of a person you really are.

Looking for a job?

Getting your LinkedIn profile accurate and attractive is one of the best ways of marketing yourself. If you can get past employers to post testimonials (LinkedIn calls them recommendations) this surely must go a long way to raising your profile and increasing your chances of getting back into a job or going after the next one.

Other key benefits of being on LinkedIn

It's your shop window; it's just like having your own personal website and, as LinkedIn and Google are closely connected, your LinkedIn profile can often be seen high up on the search engines when people search for you online. You can share your details with others and share your level 1 and indeed your level 2 contacts with others to help both parties. The first principle of networking is to be kind and generous. Using LinkedIn this way ensures you can be as effective online as offline. With your details available to all, this might help you meet people you'd never meet otherwise and it's a useful way of keeping an eye on what contacts are up to professionally. I don't mean that to sound creepy – but if Mike Smith moves to Coca-Cola and you want to get that account, this is a good way in.

"Getting your LinkedIn profile accurate and attractive is one of the best ways of marketing yourself."

PS

1. Ensure your profile is truthful, whether or not you're looking for new clients or a new role.

2. Make sure there are no typos, speeling [sic] mistakes or inaccuracies in dates and the title you had at a previous employment. As I write this, there are 263+ million people registered with LinkedIn and millions more who can check you out.

3. You want to be viewed as honest, decent and trustworthy; make certain your profile reflects this!

Chapter

3

How to prepare for the event

It's very easy to accept an invitation to an event when it's weeks or months away, but as the time approaches you might begin to feel unsure about going.

Brian's office 9:30 a.m. The day before the event. Brian finishes checking his post, switches on the computer and checks his diary.

B: *What's on today? Oh dear, it's that Premier networking evening at the Grand Hotel tomorrow. I really don't want to go. What reason can I find?*

W: *But you've said you'll go, so it's time to focus on the event tomorrow. What preparation and planning should you do?*

Don't worry about the event – one easy way to feel more in control is to prepare and plan properly. Would you ever consider having a meeting with a client or prospect without doing some preparation or planning? Of course not. Proper preparation and planning before a networking event will help to alleviate any fears you might have.

Also bear in mind that at this event you are likely to meet prospects or even existing clients, or maybe that new employer. It's really important that you're prepared, and it's easy to do if you follow a few simple steps.

"Proper preparation and planning before a networking event will help to alleviate any fears you might have."

What should you do before the event?

1. **Try to obtain a guest list**. It's not always possible to get one, but you should always ask. If it's a small event, then call the host instead to ask who's going.

2. **Identify who you should talk to**. When you get the list, read it carefully to see if there is anyone you particularly wish to talk to. Meeting one person who you'd like to talk to might make the whole event worthwhile.

3. **Find out about the guests**. Do some online research on those people and on your hosts. LinkedIn and company websites are a great resource. Not only will you find out more about what they do, but you might also discover some shared interests outside work.

4. **Get directions**. Ensure you know how to get to the venue, where to park, and which room the event is in.

5. **Don't forget your business cards**. These are key and without them you'll struggle to pass on your contact details with ease.

6. **Find out the format and dress code.** Always find out if it's a breakfast meeting, a drinks reception or ...? This way you won't be caught off guard if you're expecting to mill around a function room in your work suit, but they're actually doing a general knowledge quiz in casual clothes!

7. **Check the timings.** Know the start and finishing time. I am supposed to be a confident networker – after all I share my knowledge constantly – but I hate walking into a room which is already formed with lots of groups; so how do I avoid it? It's simple – I plan my diary to arrive there early. That way everyone else has to come in and join me. I'm there early to feel in command and control of the situation.

8. **Update yourself on current events in your industry and local and world news.** There's nothing like being prepared for small talk, so you should be ready to think of things to say if the conversation dries up.

9. **Plan for 'What do you do?'.** This is the only question you can guarantee to be asked, so make sure your answer is clear and jargon free. Saying you're an information advisor when you are a librarian will only serve to confuse!

B: *Yes, Will, that difficult question, 'What do you do?' I always struggle to answer it with any enthusiasm or conviction.*

W: *The big issue here, Brian, is most people say what they are and not what they do. 'I'm an accountant' or 'I'm a lawyer' or 'I'm a surveyor', etc. People generally don't care what you do; only what you can do for them. Try something like, 'I help my clients to ...' or 'I help my clients by ...' or 'I help my clients when ... or if...'.*

Another definition of networking is 'word-of-mouth marketing'. Marketing is all about benefits, so using the words 'help' or 'show' conveys your message more accurately. If you're an accountant and you tell people that, with no extra information, the likelihood is that they'll think of you as a boring person – and I know, because I used to be one (an accountant!). But that doesn't mean that I am boring, so why not also tell them what you do for your clients?

"Marketing is all about benefits, so using the words 'help' or 'show' conveys your message more accurately."

Instead, why not say, 'I'm an accountant. I help my clients to grow their business or save them tax.' Not only have they found out what you do, they've found out what you do for clients, plus it's clear that you're thinking of your clients.

As a general rule people don't care what you do, they only care what you could do for them.

Make sure your LinkedIn profile is up to date

Just as you've been finding out about the other attendees, most of them (hopefully!) will be looking to find out about you too. So make sure your company website and your LinkedIn page are up to date, accurate and inviting. Remember to check:

- **Job title.** Have you updated this since your last promotion?
- **Photo.** Do you have a photo and, if so, is it current? An outdated photo, if you've changed your haircut or grown a little older, can be confusing to people.

See Chapter 2 for more about how to have an exciting and attractive profile.

How to look forward to the event

1. **Get yourself into a positive mindset.** Imagine yourself walking in, head held high, shoulders back ... and smiling. Tell yourself you will enjoy this event and have some real fun. It's likely that 99 per cent of the people there are feeling as nervous as you.

2. **Believe in yourself.** Remember that you're a decent and likeable person. In addition, you're very knowledgeable about your area of expertise.

3. **Think of things you'll have in common.** Ask yourself what you have in common with other people at the event. You all travelled to get there; you are all guests of the same hosts; you are all in business or work in the same sector. These are just some topics of conversation to break the ice.

4. **Turn the event into a game.** This could even be a bit of a self-challenge: try to spot three 'ahaa' moments (see page 7) and tell yourself you won't leave until you do.

5. **Remind yourself that everyone is there to network.** People want to meet you just as much as you want to meet them. The chances of rejection are tiny.

6. **Forget about rude people.** It is unlikely to happen, but very, very occasionally you might get rejected by someone. People like this aren't worth giving a second thought to. Focus on the 99.9 per cent of pleasant and welcoming people.

7. **Pay attention.** When you do spot that 'ahaa' moment, make sure you follow it up.

B: *You know, Will, you've certainly laid a few ghosts to rest in my mind. I'm beginning to look forward to this event. Who knows, I may even find it enjoyable after all!*

W: *Great, see you tomorrow.*

PS

1. Get the guest list – knowing something about who's going puts you in control and you'll start one step ahead.

2. Find out where you're going, what you're doing and what to wear – you'll feel more uncomfortable if you're wearing the wrong clothes or you're not prepared for the event.

3. Don't arrive late – it's tempting to get there a little after the event has started, but if you get there on time (or even better, a little earlier) you'll be one of the first to arrive and you'll have time to talk to the hosts. They might also introduce you to a fellow guest, which always makes breaking the ice so much easier.

Part

2

During the event

Chapter

What to do on arrival

On arrival 6:17 p.m.

B: *Well, here I am. Will, you convinced me it was going to be fun. Huh, fun! I don't even want to go in the room. I'd like to turn around right now and go home.*

W: *Come on now, Brian. Don't be a coward. It's too late to back out now. Let me remind you of three key points:*

1. *It's likely that 99 per cent of the people here are feeling the same as you, whether it's a business-related event or social gathering. This makes you normal. Everyone is at this event for the same reason as you ... business or career. That's the first thing you have in common, but there will be other things, believe me.*

2. *You've set aside time for this event, so make the time you're spending worthwhile.*

3. *No matter how positive your mindset, there are some things it's good to know in advance, like who to approach, what to say, and how to move on. So what follows are my networking essentials.*

Last-minute nerves

In public places, such as work, meetings, or shopping, people with social anxiety feel that everyone is watching and staring at them (even though rationally they know this isn't true). The socially anxious person can't relax, 'take it easy', and enjoy themselves in public. In fact, they can never relax when other people are around. It always feels like others are evaluating them, being critical of them, or 'judging' them in some way. The person with social anxiety knows that people don't do this openly, of course, but they still feel the self-consciousness and the judgment while they are in the other person's presence. It's sometimes impossible to let go, relax, and focus on anything else except the anxiety. Because the anxiety is so very painful, it's much easier just to stay away from social situations and avoid other people.

The above is actually from the Social Anxiety Institute website in the US (**https://socialanxietyinstitute.org**). It shows that millions of people share some of these symptoms and all these fears are quite normal ... and universal.

The Social Anxiety Institute states that social anxiety is the third largest mental health problem in the US today, after alcoholism and depression.

The top ten networking fears and concerns

#1 Where do I start in this room full of strangers?

This is a completely common – and normal – fear, but the trick
is to start small and work your way up. Is there anyone else on
their own looking for someone to talk to?

One of my favourite sayings is, 'Strategy for sustained growth is
visibility'. So come on now, let's get visible.

B: *Oh my goodness, Will. Look at all these strangers … I don't think
I know anyone. I knew I shouldn't have come. Look at that man
approaching that lady over there, confidence personified.*

OK, first things first. If you feel uncomfortable entering the room, start by going and getting yourself a drink. Then find a quiet spot to stand as you take everything in. Remember, this is a safe and secure environment so it's time to get going.

All rooms of people look the same

Something I've learnt over the years is that although rooms come in different shapes and sizes, as far as the people are concerned, they will always be present in no more than six recognisable formats. Learning to recognise these formats means that you're in control of the room and you'll always have an easy way to start talking to someone.

The wallflower

You will often see a man or woman standing on their own. They of course stand at the edge of the room. They feel uncomfortable because they don't know anyone or are too nervous to approach someone new.

W: *Take that lady over there, she is mentally nailed to the floor and you know what she is doing against the wall? She's praying. What do you think she's praying for? And I'll give you a clue, it's not world peace.*

B: *For someone to go and talk to her?*

This person is an ideal starting point for you because she doesn't know any one, so probably like you, she's nervous and vulnerable. She's praying for someone to talk to her, so why shouldn't it be you? Also take into account that this is a business-related event. She wants to meet others just like you do, in fact just like everyone here tonight does.

Couples

We have highlighted the single person. Now let me introduce you to the other five groups, starting with couples. Do you notice any difference between these two couples?

The women are in a closed format, i.e. standing face to face, the men in an open stance. You know all about body language being a key channel of communication, so which couple do you think are indicating it's OK for you to come in, and which couple are saying, 'We're having a private conversation ... stay away for the moment?'

As a general rule it is less common to see men in a closed format, or women – whether with another woman or a man – in an open stance. This is because women tend to build relationships quicker than men, and if they like you then they give you their full attention by facing you. Men take longer to build relationships, and even when they do, they are far more comfortable standing in a 'V' shape or side by side, which is far less threatening and intimidating. If you see two men in a closed 'two' – watch out, there could be a fight about to start!

"Women tend to build relationships quicker than men, and if they like you then they give you their full attention by facing you."

The open couple is the one to approach, as you probably won't be interrupting a confidential conversation.

Groups of three

Now let's look at groups of threes. Have a look at these two groups. What do you notice?

B: *Ah yes. I understand. I can see the open stance with one group and the closed stance with the other. So again if I were to pick one, I should choose the open group?*

Again, read the body language before approaching. The best group to join is any group, opened or closed, where there is someone there you know. This makes it easier as hopefully the person you know will introduce you to the person or people they're talking to.

"The best group to join is any group, opened or closed, where there is someone there you know."

Groups of four or more

And last but not least, groups of four or more. These groups can appear very daunting, given how many people are involved. When you know someone in a larger group such as this, feel free to approach. Otherwise, the best advice is to stay clear.

W: *So, recap. What have you learnt so far?*

B: *Well, I guess there are only six ways that people can assemble:*

1. *The person standing on their own.*

2. *The open two.*

3. *The open three.*

4. *The closed two.*

5. *The closed three.*

6. *The larger groups of four or more standing in a circle, which will always be closed.*

Top tip

When you get your name badge, put it on your right lapel, not your left. When you wear it on the right and you shake hands, your right shoulder is thrust forward, so when you first shake hands with someone, they see it. If you wear it on the left, it's out of their line of sight and people have to strain across to view your badge.

One of the fears we have when we walk in to a room is being overwhelmed by sheer numbers; that's natural and normal. But from now on walk in, head held high and survey the room. It will be familiar and recognisable.

"From now on walk in, head held high and survey the room."

PS

1. Before you enter a room, give yourself a positive talking to and destroy those negative voices in your head.

2. Survey the room and decide who you're going to approach.

3. Find people you think you will have something in common with; for example, same gender or same age range.

Chapter

5

How to break the ice

The top ten networking fears and concerns

#2 How do I break the ice?

Making the first move is daunting, but it doesn't have to be. Follow the clear steps in this chapter to start the conversation flowing.

At the event 6:27 p.m.

W: *How are you feeling now, Brian? It's time to approach someone. So, of the six acceptable formats, who do you think will be the easiest to approach?*

B: *Hang on a moment! I don't feel great, but of the six different groups I think the person on their own would be easiest to approach.*

Meeting people is the second stage of the networking pipeline. You've accepted the invitation so now's the time to see who else has turned up to the event.

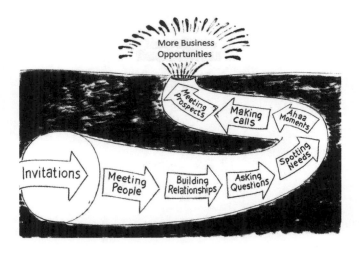

Step-by-step guide on how to move forward

You see that lady over there? It says Betty on her name badge.

She is waiting for you to talk to her. Here is what you should do:

- Walk over slowly. Remember she is nervous and knows no one – that's why she is alone.
- Stop about one metre away and smile … don't forget the smile. Ask if you can join her. You may want to use the words, 'May I join you?' or any other opening phrase that you feel comfortable with.
- Shake hands firmly, maintaining good eye contact.
- *She will not say no.* In fact, she will give you a big mental hug. Don't expect a real one, it's too soon!
- Introduce yourself with your first name only. Even if you are wearing name badges, it is usual to introduce yourself by name. Make sure you listen, and I mean truly listen, so that you hear her name. Then use it once or twice in the conversation to cement it. If someone you know then comes over, it will be easy to introduce them with no embarrassment.
- Then ask the icebreaker (see page 50) and off you go.

It sounds simple, and it is. If you feel uncomfortable about approaching a stranger, here are some ground rules that might make it easier:

- **Approach the person you think you will feel most secure with**. If you find it easier to talk to women, then start with a woman. If you find it easier to talk to men, try a man first.

- **Look for people of your own age group**. Many young people I come across find it intimidating talking to their elders as they perceive they are less knowledgeable, by comparison. So stick to people your own age, at least at the start of an event. You're bound to have more in common and therefore will feel much more comfortable.

- **Keep it short (or tall)**. As you can see, I am a little vertically challenged. So for me, going up to three people all over two metres tall makes me feel a little uncomfortable.

You don't always have a choice over who you end up talking to, but when you do, make it easy for yourself. Practise talking to strangers – even if they seem an easy choice to you. This will make you feel more at ease and you will be more prepared for others down the line.

"Practise talking to strangers – even if they seem an easy choice."

Top tip

Think: Male or female? Young or old? Tall or not so tall?

When networking, it's important to ensure you feel the best you can. In other words, network with purpose. All the work you do with clients and business contacts is thought through using all your expertise and knowledge. The networking part of your job should be tackled in the same skilled and professional manner. Even experienced networkers, including myself, take a deep breath before walking into a room and usually start off with the easy option. I will start an event talking to people I know; it makes me feel secure and relaxed. Believe me, even when you have done it many times, you will still have slight feelings of self-doubt and hesitation. My role is to ensure that those feelings are minimal.

"Even experienced networkers take a deep breath before walking into a room."

Remembering names

I'm sure everyone has at some point been introduced to someone and immediately forgotten their name. Names are critical for networking, so how do you ensure you remember them correctly?

The first thing you have to do is change your attitude to people's names. It's not a matter of your memory; you can retain all sorts of information. If I asked you to tell me five facts about, say, ten clients you are working with at this moment, you could, couldn't you? Yet at a networking event when all you have to do is to retain one or, occasionally, two words (a name!), you struggle.

The reason you forget is because you're not listening in the first place. You are so busy trying to make a good first impression you miss the most important aspect of relationship building – their name. Your name is important to you and everyone else's name is equally as important to them.

"Remembering names is a mindset, not a memory issue."

Remembering names is a mindset, not a memory issue. So stop thinking, 'I'm rubbish with names'. Instead think, 'I build better and quicker relationships when I work just a little harder at remembering people's names. I am going to treat their name with the same respect I treat the owner of that name.' So how can you remember names better?

- **Picture association**. Using pictures can help you remember. See Jane and Ken below? Ken's got the right idea. He's thinking about Tarzan's Jane swinging in an apple tree.

- **Forget surnames.** You're only interested in the first name first, so concentrate your efforts on that.

- **Repeat, repeat, repeat.** Repeat the name as you are shaking hands and concentrate on that one word. Use the name a couple of times in the early moments of the conversation to cement it in your memory.

- **Don't be embarrassed.** If you don't hear their name because it's noisy, they speak far too quickly or they have a name that is not familiar to you, then simply say, 'I'm sorry, can you tell me your name again?' They will never say, 'I've told you once, I'm not going to tell you again!!' In fact, they will be pleased you're showing such an interest.

Dale Carnegie summed it up over 80 years ago in his famous book *How to Win Friends and Influence People*: 'A person's name is to that person the sweetest and most important sound in any language.'

Top tip

So many people have limp handshakes. Ensure yours is firm but not too firm. Make sure the contact is good by fitting the semicircle between your forefinger and your thumb into theirs. And *always* make good eye contact when shaking hands.

So, back to Betty. After you have approached her, smile, ask if you can join her, shake hands properly, make eye contact and introduce yourself with your first name. She will almost certainly give her first name.

W: *This is your big moment, Brian. Focus and give your full attention to that one word. If she gives you her surname (which I happen to know is Focalpinto), ignore it.*

How to start the conversation

Now for the icebreaker. 'Please may I join you' isn't part of the conversation – think of that as simply the hors d'oeuvre. Let's go to the main course. In the list of mental exercises before entering the room, you should consider what you have in common with others. That is your icebreaker.

"Consider what you have in common with others. That is your icebreaker."

So, what do you think you have in common with Betty? There are six things which immediately come to mind:

1. You are both here at the same event.
2. You are both guests of the same company or both attending the same conference with a common interest.
3. If you approach Betty, at that moment, you are both on your own and nervous.
4. You are both in business.
5. You are here to network and meet others.
6. You both travelled to get here tonight.

The last one is the icebreaker I use any time, any place, anywhere – 'Where have you come from?' This is non-threatening and gives the other person numerous options with their answer. They may say the town, the district, the road, their company – it doesn't really matter. As long as you respond with another question or a statement, you will find they are so relieved to have someone talking to them that you receive a warm reception. Believe me, they will *never* walk off! And if they do, would that person be the sort you'd want to build a relationship with anyway?

So off you go!

PS

1. Find something in common with others attending the event to use as an icebreaker question.

2. People will always be polite to you as long as you behave in a similar fashion.

3. Remembering names is critical in building relationships.

Chapter

6

How to move on

At the event 6:42 p.m.

B: *Hi Will, I'm back … a bit battered and bruised. It went really well. When she said where she came from, I told her my brother lives in the next road and we talked about the picturesque park near where they live. We chatted about various things and then, all of a sudden, we seemed to run out of things to say and there was a long silence. We both stood there like lemons and I was beginning to feel very uncomfortable. I didn't know what to do … so I just stood there.*

W: *So why are you feeling battered and bruised?*

B: *Well, she then said, 'Brian, it's been very nice meeting you, but I think it's time to go and meet other people'. I feel sort of rejected.*

Congratulate yourself on starting a conversation – to go from feeling nervous about even approaching someone to a short chat is fantastic progress. However, if you feel the conversation ends prematurely and you come away feeling discarded, unwanted, abandoned, it can be hard to want to carry on.

This is the primary and principal reason most people don't like networking. We all hate rejection, but it's easy to overcome this feeling and move on when the conversation comes to its natural end.

"We all hate rejection, but it's easy to overcome this feeling and move on."

The top ten networking fears and concerns

#4 How do I move on after a conversation?

We've all been stuck in conversations that we want to leave, but a big worry for networkers is that you'll fail to deal politely with a stranger you just met.

How to move on graciously, respectfully and comfortably

We've agreed, no one likes rejection. We also don't like rejecting others, as we know how it feels ourselves. That is the reason you stood next to Betty, even though you knew the conversation had finished.

But when she said, 'Brian, it's been very nice meeting you, but I think it's time to go and meet other people', you felt the subtext was, 'I'm off, bored with you, I'm sure there are more interesting people here'.

So, what do we do to ensure everyone feels comfortable with the moving-on process? I can't teach you when it's time to move on, but we all know the moment. You can be confident that once you're thinking that you'd like to go, that is what your partner is thinking too.

When it's time to move on, try the following:

- **Food or drink.** 'Betty I could do with a refill', or 'I see they're serving food … would you like to join me?'
- **I've spotted someone.** 'I've seen my friend Trudie over there, would you like me to introduce you?'

- **Commit to moving on.** The key point is to move off the spot, down the room and on.

By mentioning that you've seen someone you know and asking if they want to join you, you give the other person the option of staying or going. Most of the time they want to move on, so they decline your offer. But you've been polite, courteous and haven't rejected them.

If they do come with you, you will inevitably introduce them to someone else, or they will introduce you to someone else. Whichever, there is no embarrassment ... and no rejection. I call this 'parking'!

But what if they hang on?

What happens if you take her for a drink, she's still with you, then some food, she's still with you, then you introduce her to someone and that someone moves off ... and she's still with you? You feel stuck ... really stuck!

Now the phrase I am going to ask you to use will be a life-saver, not only when you meet someone for the first time but also when you are with a client at an event or with anyone you already know. Unless they are a confident networker, they will find comfort in staying with you. But if you want to commit to being a better networker, you will probably want to move on and meet other new people.

So if you feel stuck – here's the key phrase: 'Come on Betty (or Mary or John ...), let's go and meet some others.' Simply take them with you, and include them.

Aim for an open group of two or three and say, 'Please may we join you?' All of a sudden you are in a closed group of four or five. Everyone introduces everyone else and at that moment you have tied Betty into this new larger group. You've done your charity work for the evening! It's time to move on when you're ready.

"Networking is easy when you know how, but only when you practise."

Networking is easy when you know how, but only when you practise. These tips and ideas work every time for me, but unless you implement them next time you go networking, that's all they'll be, tips and ideas.

Introducing one person to another

If you're talking to someone you've just met and someone you know comes along, introduce both parties and explain what jobs they each have.

When you introduce one person to another, aim to say interesting and relevant facts about each person. This way you get them chatting and it gives you the opportunity to move on or turn it into a three-way conversation.

PS

1. 'Dumping' someone can often leave a bad taste; after all, you're there to build relationships, not ruin them from the start. Treat people as you want to be treated and remember people never forget how you have made them feel.

2. 'Parking' is acceptable by offering options. If they don't want to follow you, that's fine, but you have been courteous and polite and that is the key principle of networking.

3. Leave every encounter hoping they think of you as someone they might like to meet again.

Chapter

7

Dealing with groups

Moving on from groups

As you may be beginning to realise, there are simple techniques for every little move, so let me share some straightforward thinking for this area. When you and everyone else are in a group, it's made up of three types. There is the speaker, the primary listeners and the secondary listeners.

If you're the speaker, it's unlikely that you'll want to leave. And if you're the primary listener, i.e. the one interested in what the speaker has to say, again, you won't want to leave. But if you're the secondary listener, i.e. have no real interest in the conversation, it's time to move on.

To move on, simply make eye contact with all the members in the group and say, 'Please will you excuse me, I've just seen Antony over there', and off you go. If you don't know anyone in the room, just say that you're going for a drink or some similar reason.

Don't feel that you're rejecting the group – you're not leaving one person on their own, and you've done it politely so none of them are really going to be bothered.

The top ten networking fears and concerns

#5 How do I approach groups?

It's easy to start talking to one person, but to approach a group of people can seem like madness. But there are easy and straightforward tips to ensure you do it right.

Approaching groups

Nervous networkers often feel isolated in a room full of strangers, and seeing other people in groups or talking to others can make this feel worse. But if you can join a new group then this feeling will stop. So here's how.

We talked earlier, in detail, about approaching singles, but now it's time to touch on those occasions where you have to approach a group, and this time you're on your own.

Approaching groups of two or three can seem scary, and it's not as simple as approaching a person on their own, but it's still straightforward. It's also necessary, because if you do arrive a little late and there are no singles, approaching a group is your only option.

> **Top tip**
>
> Most people go to an event and spend the whole time with people they know. Reinforcing existing relationships is great, but you won't meet any new people, and this is often why people feel they've wasted their time.

Don't feel inclined to just talk to people you know because it's easy. I want you to talk to known associates and contacts, but not to the exclusion of meeting new people. You need to find a balance between existing and potential new contacts, which means stepping out of your comfort zone.

"Find a balance between existing and potential new contacts, which means stepping out of your comfort zone."

What I usually do is spend time at the beginning of the event talking to people I know. That way, I've done the pleasantries and done some relationship maintenance. But once that's done, it's time to meet new people and look for the 'ahaa' moments (as mentioned in Chapter 1).

All you need to do is simply go up to a group and ask permission to join. It's just like approaching the singles, but there are a few points to remember. When we talked about breaking the ice, I mentioned the issues of gender, age and height – maybe that last one is just for me but I doubt it. All groups will of course be made up of some or all of those types. For example, you see that group just to your left. It's made up of two men and a woman … a good group to approach.

It's a mixed-gender group and the women are usually the friendly ones and will welcome you in. My advice to everyone is to try and find a mixed-gender group, as the 'opposite sex' will be more welcoming. If a woman approaches a men-only group, the chances of being warmly welcomed will be greater.

"Try and find a mixed-gender group, as the 'opposite sex' will be more welcoming."

But I repeat. The mixed-gender group, from my vast experience, is safest for all of us. Before approaching, think which group will 'suit you'. If you are in a jovial mood and you see a happy set, move towards them. When you are in your serious mode, maybe a quieter group will be better for you. Don't make it harder than it needs to be; that's my simple message.

Once you have spotted your chosen group, approach slowly, aiming to catch the attention of the person talking. Stop just at the edge of the group, smile and say to the person talking – as it is that person you are actually interrupting – either, 'Excuse me, please may I join you?' and maybe add, 'I don't know anyone here tonight and you seem to be a fun group'. As you are saying this, ensure you scan the group with your eyes to show you are engaging with each person.

Networking is an inclusive activity, not an exclusive one. Bear in mind that it's highly unlikely they'll say, 'No push off' or, 'Get lost, we don't want losers around here, thank you'. The chances of rejection are remote, so don't worry.

What will normally happen is the people on the edge step back and their shoulders move to face you. They will nearly always say, 'Of course, my name is John, this is Mary and this is Peter'. Listen hard to remember their names, and repeat their names in turn. Remember that you're absolutely capable of remembering three words, it's just a mindset.

So, once you are in, you are in and you can be involved in the group. However don't take over the conversation; start as a secondary listener before getting fully involved.

Playing host

> **Top tip**
>
> Even when you are a guest at an event – think host.

When you host an event, at home or through business, you're expected to welcome people, make them feel comfortable, introduce one guest to another, not to mention, amongst other things, offering them a drink and some food.

When you think host, you act in a different way, more confident, more purposeful, and more certain. For example, just look at that group over there.

It looks like a group of four, but in fact there are only three in the group; the fourth person is standing on his own. How do you think the fourth man is feeling?

Bearing in mind what I have just said about hosting, what do you think should happen next? The group should invite him to join them. Then he'll feel fantastic! And you know something else? They are probably ready to 'freshen up' the conversation and bringing a new member into the group will achieve that.

So, if you ever find yourself in that situation, i.e. if you are in a group and see someone 'loitering' nearby, invite them in and play host. After the introductions say, 'We were just talking about the latest ...'. That way you give your new entrant an opportunity to participate in the conversation.

How to approach closed groups

B: *You know something, Will, it's all beginning to fall into place now. And I've just spotted someone I know in that group over there. Laura, the woman with the glasses.*

W: *A group like that with people you know and people you don't is a superb format. Laura over there obviously knows those people now, so it will be so much easier to get in there using Laura as your entry.*

As I said previously, you should generally avoid closed groups (where people are all facing inwards), but if you know someone in the group it's a great opportunity to get involved.

Remember this about networking: in the business world there are two individuals who are useful in business. Those you know and those you want to know. If you know someone in a group, but don't know any of the others, this is a great way to meet the people you want to know through the people you do know.

"There are two individuals who are useful in business. Those you know and those you want to know."

If you know Laura well, simply approach the group, sidle up to Laura and gently ask, 'Laura, may I join you?' As you know each other well, it's likely she will step aside, let you in and introduce you to the others.

> **PS**
>
> 1. Life's too short to waste time in groups where you have nothing to contribute or you have no interest in the topic under discussion. Simply excuse yourself and leave.
>
> 2. Where it is obvious someone you're talking to isn't interested and behaves badly by looking over your shoulder, read the body language and do them and yourself a favour … move on.
>
> 3. When you attend events it generally means you've extended your working day and deprived friends, family and your hobbies and interests of your attention. Those times are precious; don't waste them.

Chapter

8

Managing rejection

The top ten networking fears and concerns

#6 How will I manage rejection?

Getting ignored is admittedly the worst moment in networking: when you approach that group and they basically ignore you and continue their conversation. You've done everything right; you've thought all about the make-up in the group, ensured it's an open-formatted one and then the big comedown. This chapter looks at how to get over rejection and move on.

Coping with rejection, rudeness and bad manners

B: *But what happens if I approach a group and they just ignore me? Don't tell me it will never happen.*

W: *Brian, I can't promise it will never happen; all I am saying is it will be rare.*

Here's how to overcome your (and everyone else's) nightmare. Firstly, think about who you are:

- You're a decent, agreeable and likeable person.
- You have been polite and courteous in your approach to this group.
- You have aimed to make the right impression.
- You have an expertise and are well qualified in what you do.
- You know lots of people who you can introduce – perhaps some of them are at the event.

- You plan on being a good listener rather than taking over the conversation.

- You hope that you and your organisation have a good name and provide an excellent service to your existing clients.

Having thought about all of the above, who do you think should be feeling bad at the moment, you or them? They have behaved rather rudely, so take the moral high ground and move off as soon as you can. Think as many rude thoughts as you like, but keep your composure and poise. This bit is hard, but say something like, 'I'm really sorry but I seem to have interrupted a private conversation, I'll leave you to carry on'. It might feel hard to say, but it's better than waiting for one of them to acknowledge you. Because every second you stand there being ignored will seem like a lifetime!

Let me talk to you about rudeness and bad manners. I can't say you won't come across such behaviour, but it won't happen too often. In life and at work, most people are nice. They're also usually pleasant, friendly, well mannered and polite. Accept this, so when you walk into that scary room, you'll be reassured.

"Most people are nice. Accept this, so when you walk into that scary room, you'll be reassured."

There will be times when you are talking to Gary and Dave comes over. Dave knows Gary but doesn't know you. Dave ignores you and starts talking to Gary. Gary, of course, is generally embarrassed and doesn't introduce you … but probably only because he has forgotten your name! If this happens, introduce yourself at a suitable moment … or excuse yourself, if you have been ignored for more than five seconds. The chances are by then Gary will somehow find a way to include you into the conversation.

This brings me to another little technique to ensure no one ever accuses you of impoliteness. When you are in the bigger group and you're the speaker, there is always a secondary listener

– remember the person who isn't directly involved in the conversation? The best way to invite that person to participate is, when you're talking, to glance at that person, indicating you acknowledge that they are still there. That gives them the option of contributing or not.

In networking situations if people feel stuck in a group but don't know how to get away, there are often lots of secondary listeners all thinking, 'How do I get away from here?' But if you include them they probably won't want to go because they feel included.

Networking isn't scary. It's all about respect, courtesy and consideration for the feelings of others. Good manners is good business and bad manners often mean no business. We forget what people have said or done to us, but we don't forget how people make us feel.

"Networking isn't scary. It's all about respect, courtesy and consideration for the feelings of others."

Read their body language

Consider the people who look over their shoulder or glance around the room when they're talking to you. What is their body language saying? They're saying they feel disinterested, so it's time to move on.

When the conversation comes to a lull, simply say, 'Well Jack, it's been good talking to you, will you excuse me? I have just seen Jill over there, I promised I'd catch up with her.' Or use the drink, food, or, last but not least, even the toilet excuse. Remember you're not rejecting them, because they are looking for a get-out too. They have probably found you immensely interesting but want to move on, and don't know how to do it in a polite manner. Whatever it is they are thinking, leaving them means they are going to feel mightily relieved. But you have kept your dignity and decorum and behaved in a perfect manner.

PS

1. If they're honest, everyone will admit they have a fear of rejection, even though rejection rarely happens.

2. If a group doesn't welcome you in, move away instantly.

3. Some people just don't want to talk to you. This is fine! Get over it ... and quickly!

Chapter

9

Building relationships

The event 7:05 p.m.

B: Hi, Will, I'm back. Laura was very welcoming and friendly, but she didn't introduce me to the others. But I asked her if I could introduce myself and I met Melanie, Celia, Joanne and Robert.

W: Fantastic – you know she probably didn't introduce the other people because she couldn't remember their names. By asking to introduce yourself, she was probably mightily relieved and tremendously grateful. Why? Because you got her out of a big hole, saving her a lot of embarrassment.

Let's go back to the networking pipeline now, and look at the third stage, building relationships.

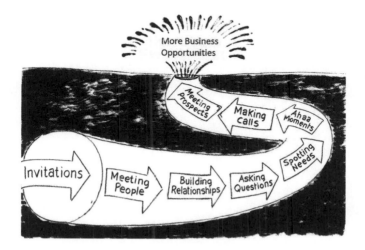

This is really important as it's building relationships that makes the difference between missing and getting new business.

Once you've broken the ice with people and started talking, it can suddenly seem that you've drifted into talking about random topics, such as breeding hamsters or scuba diving. This might seem frivolous or inappropriate, given it's a business event, but don't worry.

Small talk before business talk

It might seem that you wasted a good opportunity to get down to business, but actually this kind of conversation is great. You've met Claire and even though knowing she has two kids called Peter and Molly, plus a dog called Rover, might seem useless, it is in fact relationship building. The fact that you've come away with this information means the conversation went well – firstly, you made a great impression on Claire and she won't forget that. Secondly finding some common topic can really build a strong relationship. Will it turn into business? Who knows, but remember this: everyone is somebody's somebody, so even if the person you're talking to has no need for your services they may know someone who does.

The top ten networking fears and concerns

#7 How can I make myself interesting and exciting?

When people ask, 'What do you do?' in your work life, aim to explain what benefits you bring to your existing clients rather than telling them what your job title is. People don't care what you do, only what you can do for them.

So how do you gauge whether a conversation is going well? It might seem that some people only want to talk about themselves. They tell you about their job, their company, their last holiday and their children. They don't allow you to escape, by standing in a closed format, and you feel unable to move on. If this happens, remember how to move on successfully – say you've spotted someone or you want a drink, and ask if they want to join you.

It's all about the questions

People love talking about themselves, and your key role is to let them. Let the other person do most of the talking; be a good listener and encourage others to talk about themselves. We learn nothing when we talk, only when we listen.

"We learn nothing when we talk, only when we listen."

Even if the other person hasn't learnt anything about you, you've learnt lots, and it might not be useful now, but it could be useful in the future. Giving your full attention to them makes them feel good and that's a great beginning to any relationship. Networking is about giving, and the greatest gift one individual can give to another is their full attention.

Now you know what they do, you can bear in mind whether their role (and company) is a good fit for you and your company. Who knows when you may be able to do business together? If you decide you'd like to build a relationship with a view to potential future business, then you need to follow up and keep in touch, and I'm sure they won't forget you.

Don't forget, we're only here to build relationships – the start of the three stages of knowing, liking and trusting. If you get to stage 1 (knowing), but don't want to get to stage 2 (liking), then nothing will happen and there's nothing to worry about.

If you only come away with two or three 'ahaa' moments at the end of any event, you've made good use of your time.

The core skills of effective networkers are:

- asking pertinent questions
- listening attentively
- looking for the 'ahaa' moment and acting on it where relevant.

Let me reiterate the sorts of people who make effective networkers. It's not the loud, apparently self-confident ones who appear to be the life and soul of the party. It's often the quieter ones who ask good questions, listen and follow up. You'll never see me 'working the room'. I talk quietly one-to-one or in groups, looking for openings, information and knowledge.

When you actually see people working the room, they probably won't be doing it effectively. They'll be flitting from one person to another, handing out loads of business cards, without really having any meaningful conversations.

Once you feel more confident in a group situation, you might occasionally get into bad habits by spending more time being interesting. If you hear yourself talking too much, think of the following two acronyms:

- **WAIT**: 'Why am I talking?'
- **STALL**: 'Stop talking and listen and learn'.

> **Top tip**
>
> If you feel that you're only talking about yourself, think WAIT and get back on track. Change the conversation and say, 'Enough about me, tell me about your hamsters'.

The top ten networking fears and concerns

#8 How do I keep the conversation going?

People often struggle to keep a conversation going after the first few moments, but let me now share the varied topics to use if you really do want to build rapport and find out about this new person. The generic phrase for these topics is 'small talk'.

Small talk

Small talk can feel uncomfortable and unnatural when you don't know people very well, but it's vitally important. You can't do big business without the small talk, so although it might not seem like business is being discussed, you are building a solid foundation for your business relationship.

"You can't do big business without the small talk."

People like people who are like them and who like, or dislike, the same things. Think of football team supporters, or the local tennis club members. We're all in 'clubs' and when we have the same focus or common interests, that helps with the bonding. Even hamster owners will enjoy networking when they talk hamsters!

Here's one trick I've learnt over the years – women are generally better at building relationships than men. Women have a whole range of topics to talk about, but some men tend to have two topics, both beginning with 'F': football ... and football.

Here's a simple system for small talk to ensure you don't run out of steam again. Next time the conversation stalls, but you feel you would like to stay with the person, use the following system to help you jump-start or rekindle the conversation. This 30-second exercise could make a massive difference.

W: *Brian, have a hard look at this picture. What do you see?*

B: *Hey, that's me, looking across the road at my neighbour's house. There's a business card and flying through – it is an aeroplane with tennis racquets for propellers. Why is there a newspaper on the pilot's seat? Oh and look there's Vicky, Mel and Rosemary, my neighbour's three children.*

This picture might look odd – but for Brian it represents the key symbols he can use in a conversation:

- **The house.** This is a symbol for asking questions like, 'Where do you live?' 'Where do you come from?' 'Have you travelled far?' 'Do you live in the city, or in the country?' 'Tell me about the area you grew up in.' When tuning into people's roots and where they spent their formative years, listen out for accents. When I meet people who aren't obviously born in my region I comment and ask if they live locally now or are they just visiting.

- **The business card.** This is to remind Brian to ask questions about what people do, where they work, etc.

- **The aeroplane.** This is a symbol for questions on the subject of holidays, business travel, how they got here tonight, etc.

- **Tennis racquets.** These are to remind Brian to talk about interests, hobbies, even the dreaded football.

- **The newspaper.** This reminds Brian to ask about current events.

- **The family.** This represents Brian's social side. A word of warning on family: it's generally not ideal to talk about family very early on in the building of relationships. When people don't have children, or someone has just separated or divorced, it may be an aspect of their life they don't wish to talk about. But when the other person talks about their spouse or children, that's your green light. All I suggest is that you don't initiate the topic, as it could potentially get embarrassing or awkward. Mention your circumstances, so that where there is common ground they can often share their personal situation. Never ask directly, 'Are you married?' or 'Do you have a family?'

So, for your small talk, create a similar sort of picture in your mind to help you think of things to say. Remember, it's best not to talk business immediately but do keep it at the back of your mind because this is a business event.

Now I speak generally of course, but at these events, men often tend to stick to sport and business. Women cover all the other topics but often leave out the topic of business. They'd rather spend longer building the relationship; the business can come later. Men tend to go straight in. Women sometimes admit that when they meet another woman and start with the small talk, they realise on their way home they never actually got on to the topic of business.

If you do spot an 'ahaa' moment, a good way forward is to swap business cards and ask them to get in touch. But you can become far more proactive than that, and we'll get on to that soon.

The top ten networking fears and concerns

#9 When do I move from the small talk to business?

To build rapport quickly it is always best to start with non-business topics and if possible find some common ground. It can't always happen because if the other person gets their 'What do you do?' question in first then it starts immediately with business.

Talking business

Generally men don't do small talk, so if a woman talks to a man and she wants to go straight to business, that's fine. But if you meet a woman who wants to talk more generally, then go with the flow.

The topic of business

The only way you find out about people's businesses and their business challenges – and everyone has them – is to ask questions. You can't create need, you can only spot potential opportunities. We all want more – or less – of something; we want to start doing something new or stop doing something tiresome or repetitive.

> **"The only way you find out about people's businesses and their challenges is to ask questions."**

If you were to think about your business's current challenges, then it's likely you have crazy busy times and then slack periods where you and the team are scratching around for things to do. This is common to everyone, and most businesses in the professional, financial and technical arenas have the same issues.

And it's simply because you are relying on referrals and existing clients, coming back for more, to decide when you will be busy or not. Think of your existing clients and contacts as a tank. However good you are, every day clients drip out. They sell out, merge, retire, even die; they don't need your services any longer, and those events are totally outside your control. On top of that, you get clients trickling away through dissatisfaction, be it service or cost.

Topping up this tank, or just keeping it at the same level, means you have to be in charge. At the moment you have probably left this control in the hands of others. If you want to develop and expand, you simply can't continue depending on introducers and existing clients coming back for more.

It's simply a case of getting out meeting new people and making new contacts of your own. In other words, become more pro-active and stop waiting for things to happen.

Here we come to the fourth stage of the networking pipeline: asking questions.

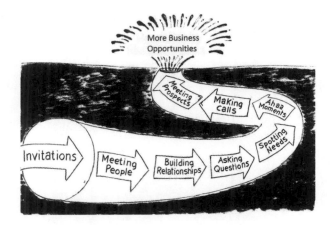

This is your chance to (gently) find out more about the person you've just met, and how you might work together in the future.

Looking for the 'ahaa' moments

Everyone in business is faced with challenges at some point, so when you're talking to someone at an event, it's good to try and establish what those issues are. Whilst I am not expecting you to go to events with a mental clipboard containing a series of pre-prepared questions, the following are question techniques to consider:

- **The open question**. These questions tend to begin with words such as *who, what, why, when, which, how,* etc. These questions get your new contact to talk freely and for you to establish the facts.

- **The closed question**. Here, you control the discussion and confirm the facts. For example, 'Are you busy this year?'

- **The clarifying question**. You review what you've heard and check your understanding of what has been said. For example, 'Why exactly do you think your business is doing so well?'
- **The probing question**. Here you can explore a comment in more detail and focus on detail. For example, 'Tell me more about the state of your industry.'

Business people who set up from scratch, are often self-centred, proud, positive and confident, and often rightly so. They have created something from nothing; they give people employment, build wealth for themselves and people around them (their suppliers). Always get in the question: 'How did you get into that?'

Anyone who is successful, either as an entrepreneur or someone high up in corporate life, can be quite challenging. These people love to talk about their achievements, their dreams. Great. Let them. They will love you. It can be hard sometimes, but if the person you're talking to is your market, keep asking the right questions and keep listening for the important information, the 'ahaa' moment. For further detailed business questions see Chapter 10.

If you come in too strong too fast, you probably won't get any future business. When you see an opportunity (the 'ahaa' moment) this is the actual starting place for your follow-up.

This is a bad time however to go into selling mode. Don't say how good, how big, how expert etc. your company is. That's selling. Instead, once you've spotted the opportunity, ask for their business card. That small piece of paper is your passport to potential business; your golden ticket to the Willy Wonka factory, your gateway to potential riches. I could go on.

PS

1. The most interesting people we ever meet are those who are most interested in us. Ensure you are that interesting person.

2. Finding common ground through small talk is the key to building rapport.

3. Asking intelligent and searching business questions will mean you may sometimes spot a potential business opportunity for your services and products.

Chapter

10

Asking business questions

The key skill of the effective networker is the ability to ask relevant and intelligent questions. Conversations are made up of two areas: the small talk, which builds relationships and rapport, and discussions about people's business and their careers.

People buy people before they buy the product or service. And that is where many people go wrong; they go into selling mode too quickly.

"People buy people before they buy the product or service."

Networking means building relationships. We attend business events to start new relationships or to reinforce existing ones, and once we are there we engage. Networking? It used to be called talking before the word came into vogue.

When you want to spot a potential business opportunity so you can share your knowledge, expertise and experience with prospects (let's call it selling!), you have to establish a want or need. You can't create a need, but you can discover a possible opportunity for mutually beneficial business.

Your guidelines to asking questions

Before I suggest some questions you might like to try asking, consider the following:

- Don't turn your questioning into an interrogation; make sure it is simply a conversation. Think fishing, not harpooning!

- You will meet two types of people. First are people who are happy to share all sorts of facts with you; we call them the 'high reactor'. Then there are the 'low reactor' types; these people are cautious and maybe even suspicious of someone they're meeting for the first time. You have to identify quickly which personality you're conversing with.

- Concentrate on asking open-formatted questions, which should start with the words *who, what, why, when, where, which* and *how* (see Chapter 9). Even the low reactor then has to answer you in a sentence rather than just saying 'yes' or 'no'.

- When someone says something you don't understand, or if you want more information, don't pretend you know. Probe and clarify to discover more. Use six words to gain more information: '*Tell* me what you mean; *explain* how that works; *describe* that in more detail; what do you mean by that *exactly*?; where in *particular* does that fit into the equation?; how *specifically* does it work?'

The sequential order of your questions

Whilst I don't want to suggest everyone asks the same questions in the same order, I do believe it is worth discovering what you need to know in a chronological order, and the following time line is useful for this:

1. Their present situation.
2. Their past history.
3. Their future plans.

The reason I suggest this is that if you don't invest enough time knowing about their 'now' or their past, you cannot possibly gain enough information to know if you or your business can help them. And by jumping too quickly to their future it shows you're not really that interested in who they are, and you could well be accused of selling – and that would be far too early in the relationship-building process.

The business timeline

Now

Top tip

In the early part of the conversation, always start with the 'now'. The obvious opener is, 'What do you do?'.

Let's listen in to a conversation between Tom and Brian.

B: So Tom, what do you do? (*Open*)

T: I'm in engineering, Brian.

B: What *particular* type of engineering? (*Probing*)

T: We specialise in making stainless steel flanges.

B: Flanges? Oh dear I don't know what that is. *Tell* me, what's a flange? (*Open*)

T: It's a fitting which goes between two pipes to keep them together.

B: *Explain* to me what happens to these flanges. (*Open*)

T: They end up in food-processing factories.

B: Is that your only target market? (*Closed*)

T: No, we are supplying them to the drinks and brewing industry, but only a few.

B: So, how are you finding business at the moment, Tom? (*Open*)

T: Well, Brian, business is going well. We're extremely busy, can't cope with the demand, I'm glad to say.

B: That sounds great. Have you identified the *specific* reason for that success?

T: Yes, we have built a reputation for reliability. We very rarely let our customers down with deliver dates and when we know we aren't going to hit the deadline we warn them well in advance.

B: Sounds impressive, Tom. *Tell* me where you are based. (*Open*)

T: We have two main sites. The head office and research department is in the city of Aye and the factory is on the main road between Aye and Bee, you know the big industrial estate on the A123?

B: Yes, I know that. Are you a big company? (*Closed*) (*Tip: try asking this closed question in an open manner.*)

B: How big a company are you? (*Open*) (*Tip: this is better, but 'big' doesn't tell you too much. It's always important to establish size and scale. You need to know if the person's business fits into your target market or, if you're looking for a job, whether or not it is the right size for your next role. The following is a better question.*)

B: How many people work in the company?

T: Oh we employ about 250 staff, Brian.

B: What do you do in the company, Tom? (*Tip: very early, find out what the other person's role is. The sooner you establish that the more pertinent questions you can ask.*)

T: I'm the production director of the company, Brian.

Once you have established if it is your target industry, the right size of company and you are talking to a senior(ish) person, it's time to get focused! It is at this point you can start to ask more personal questions about the person as well as the business.

- What do you feel about …?
- What does it mean to you if …?
- What are the implications of …?
- What do you get out of …?
- Am I right in thinking …?
- How important is …?
- Why do you value …?
- What do you think would happen if …?
- How do you feel about …?

- What are your views on ...?
- What if ...?
- What is the most important thing to you about ...?
- That's interesting. Why is that?
- What is the most frustrating thing to you about ...?

The past

Let's go back to Brian and Tom:

B: So, Tom. How did you get into engineering?

T: Well, I've been doing it since I left university. My father was in the same profession so it was natural I followed.

B: And how did you get started on your own? (*Tip: when you meet someone who has set up their own business, always ask how they got started. They will love telling you the story of their success and you will become very popular.*)

T: Well that is an interesting story ...

Although it is important to establish the 'now' and some history, what is now and what has passed can't be changed. It is the future where there is the possible opportunity to do business or get a job with the person you're talking to. People will only make changes when something different happens in their business or personal life. If a person's situation is static, there is generally no need for change. Part of your role is to ascertain if they have any changes coming up or if they are dissatisfied with their present advisors or suppliers.

The future

So, it's to the future you direct your questions. Have a think about using the following openings:

B: Tom, where do you see your business going in the next 18 months?

or:

B: Describe to me what you would like your company to look like in three years?

> **T:** We are hoping to expand and double the size of the company over the next five years, but within two we hope to find a company to acquire, then move the whole operation on to one site.

Top tip

If you're someone looking for your next position or you work in the professional or finance world, it could well be tempting to go into 'selling mode'. Don't. Just keep asking questions to focus on the other person.

With an answer like that, try to find out:

- what their timescale is;
- where they hope to move to;
- if they have a company in sight;
- what challenges they will have with all these major changes;
- who their advisors are and what the relationship is;
- whether they are looking to take on more employees.

However, a word of caution – never ask the last two questions unless you are with a 'high reactor' and you feel they are sharing lots of information with you about their business and its future.

The relationship with their existing advisors

You are attending a business event and everyone is looking for their 'ahaa' moment – their business opportunity – so try to feel comfortable about the next phase in the conversation. You are now building to the big moment. You've found out about them, you have ascertained it's your market and they know what you do. Let's look back at Tom and Brian for a moment:

> **B:** So Tom, do you mind if I ask, who do you use for your professional advice at the moment?

T: We use Assure and Caution.

B: I know that firm but I don't know anyone there. How long have you been with them?

T: About eight years.

B: What sort of services do they provide?

T: Oh, they just do my yearly tax stuff and annual accounts.

B: What made you choose them, Tom?

T: Well, Brian, I was recommended to them by my friend Lynda.

The next question is the core of the conversation. Now is the moment to give it everything. Use both ears and both eyes. Watch and listen to the answer. People can lie with words, but rarely with body language and tone of voice. Depending on the way they answer, you will be able to establish whether there is an opportunity.

The obvious question for Brian to ask would be:

B: Are you happy with them?

or:

B: Are they any good?

But a closed-formatted question such as this would put Tom in an awkward spot. He will not readily admit having the wrong advisors, so Brian may not get the accurate answer. Instead, Brian should try something like:

B: How do you find them then, Tom?

He will get one of two answers. First:

T: My advisors are fantastic, I'm very pleased with them. (*If you get an answer like this, don't switch off, keep probing.*)

B: I'm glad to hear that, Tom. What do they do particularly well for you? (*Remember networking is a long game. Just because Tom is satisfied today doesn't mean it will always be so.*)

Second:

> **T:** My advisor is OK. I don't really understand what he does. I just leave it to him. (*This is a neutral answer. Brian needs to go further.*)
>
> **B:** Would you recommend him to others, Tom?
>
> **T:** We feel they are not as good as they used to be, Brian. (*At this moment Brian may be thinking, 'Ahaa! This is why I attended tonight; we're going to do business.' He needs to take care he doesn't go into selling mode or he will scare off this potential prospect. If he thinks the relationship isn't as good as it should be, he should go for another question.*)
>
> **B:** If there's one thing you'd like them to do differently, what would it be?

or:

> **B:** What is it you're looking for from your professional advisors?

or, if they are really not happy, Brian could ask, in a gentle tone:

> **B:** Why are you still with them?

The key is just to listen and keep probing. Don't criticise the competition and don't start comparing your business.

Moving the relationship forward

If you do spot a true 'ahaa' moment, swap business cards and ask permission to contact them further after the event. Explain that now isn't the time to discuss their business or a job opportunity in detail. Aim to get their consent to call them, rather than email. That will be when you can find out even more about their business, their challenges and issues. It will only be during the call, or better still at a meeting, that you will ascertain if you can match your knowledge, expertise and experience to their needs and wants.

You attend events (i.e. go networking) to create a platform to start a true business relationship. Business is rarely done at the event itself. You are there to explore and discover more; timing is everything. If you go into your pitch too soon you will more than likely destroy the business relationship you went there to create.

"Business is rarely done at the event itself. You are there to explore and discover more."

When you have asked all the questions and think your service or product may fit the needs of a prospect, then you must follow up. This is not to sell, but to offer support to help the other party with the development of their business.

PS

1. Be self-assured, but don't be overconfident.
2. Behave with decorum and propriety.
3. Look out for 'ahaa' moments but don't go into selling mode.

Chapter

How to move forward

So you're having a conversation with someone, when you hear something that makes you believe that you can build on this initial relationship. Avoid the mistake of diving in and telling them how wonderful and experienced your organisation is, how you are the only people suitable, etc. Remember, you are not here to sell your firm as such; you are here to sell *you*. The rest comes later.

"Remember, you are here to sell *you*."

Getting the timings right

When you spot your 'ahaa' moment, be patient and take your time to develop the relationship to avoid coming across as pushy. Instead use follow-up as the opportunity to find out more. But what is the right way to do this? You face a dilemma when following up:

The first thing to do is to ask permission to contact your new prospect. Let me give you an example. Say you meet Emma, who owns a printing company. She's doing really well but she explains that she wants to expand. You've ascertained that, whilst she is happy with her existing advisors, she believes they are too small to advise on an acquisition. That is your 'ahaa' moment. *You must ask the question.* Otherwise you'll just be like those two over there.

They're the networking criminals. See the smiles on their faces? They've obviously heard something to their advantage. But will they do anything about it afterwards? Most don't.

I suggest you ask Emma the following:

> Emma, do you remember a few moments ago you said you thought your present advisors couldn't cope with the potential purchase of a new business? How do you feel about me calling you next week to find out more about your business, and perhaps we can meet to explore ideas?

Watch the body language and listen carefully for her answer. If it is less than positive, do say, 'Emma, if you'd rather call me, let me give you my card. Or maybe I can keep in touch by email?' No one likes to be sold to, and you don't want to start the relationship off on the wrong foot.

The follow-up is all about pace and intervals of contact. If Emma says something like, 'This is a very busy time of year for us, so it's not a good time', the opportunity has not gone forever. People won't do business unless they are:

- ready
- willing
- able.

"The follow-up is all about pace and intervals of contact."

Even though everything has gone well, we just don't know what's in the other person's mind at that moment, so it's best to back off. As far as I'm concerned, the opportunity hasn't gone forever, it just means – not yet. The next day send Emma an email saying how much you enjoyed meeting her and say that if she thinks you can help with her expansion plans, here is your direct dial number. Offer your mobile number if you believe the opportunity is big enough!

Then, when you think the time is right – each time will be different –invite her to something (but don't leave it too long). Alternatively send her something relevant to her issue – anything positive – which will ensure you won't be forgotten.

Now back to asking Emma if you can get in touch again. Where there is no negative body language, the following conversation could take place:

> **E:** Yes, Brian I'd be happy to hear from you.
>
> **B:** That's great, Emma. Could I call you, say, Tuesday or Wednesday next week?

It's best not to offer to call the next morning. It suggests you're perhaps short of work and, well, I believe it's just too soon. You should get this sort of reply:

> **E:** Yes, I think that will be fine. It's Thursday evening now, I am away for the weekend, Monday catching up, Tuesday in meetings, and so next Wednesday will be good.
>
> **B:** Going anywhere nice for the weekend?
>
> **E:** Yes, it's my silver wedding anniversary and we're going to Bruges. Ever been there?
>
> **B:** No, but I believe it's beautiful. It's called 'the Venice of the North' or something similar. In Belgium, right?
>
> **E:** You know as much about it as me, Brian!

Remember you have her card in your hand at this moment. Get out your pen and say, 'Because I don't want to forget, do you mind if I write down Wednesday, the agreed date, on the back of your card? That way I won't forget.' Do it in full view of your prospect. This shows commitment, a sort of arranged appointment almost, but most important of all, she will be expecting your call. You will see how vital this part of the follow-up is later.

Top tip

If you think they are happy to hear from you again, ask your prospect permission to call, agree the day and write it down in their sight so they know to expect you.

You are at your most popular when you've been genuinely interested, so make the most of it. Whether there is just the switchboard number or, in addition, a direct dial and a mobile number, ask which is the best number to use.

When you have built some relationship and rapport, you will usually be advised as to the best way of making contact. Avoiding gatekeepers will make your life much easier!

Avoiding the hard sell

When you spot the 'ahaa' moment, it's important to find out as much as possible about the opportunity, but without being too pushy. You want to find out your client's needs so you're best placed to answer them, but you must do it gently.

When you meet people and they're not what I call 'high reactors,' I wouldn't get into a dialogue about their present situation. Remember, always watch the body language and listen for the tone of voice when they answer your questions. We can all lie with our words, but not with our bodies and voices.

"Always watch the body language and listen for the tone of voice."

Questions to ask include:

- Do you mind me asking if you use professional advisors like us?
- So, how do you find them?

There will be many occasions where there isn't a definite opportunity, but you feel you'd like to keep in touch anyway. Simply say, 'Perhaps I can call you over the next couple of weeks to explore ideas and possibly we can get together?' That way, it leaves the door open. When you do call, you can always refer to the first get-together you had at the networking event ... or even the party.

PS

1. It's a cliché, but practise, practise, practise and networking will soon become second nature.

2. When you spot an opportunity to grow a relationship, don't waste it. You have attended the event for such an eventuality, so not to capitalise on it makes no sense at all.

3. If after getting in touch they decide not to move forward, don't take it personally. They are not rejecting you, just the offer of a business opportunity.

Part

3

After the event/following up

Chapter

12

Reviewing your new connections

Next morning 9.13 a.m.

B: *Hey that was a good do last night. Boy, am I glad I went. Right, let's put those business cards in a drawer and I'll deal with them this afternoon. Down to work ...*

W: *Morning Brian, Will here again. Can I give you some advice about what you may consider doing NOW?*

Even if the event was worth attending, the next morning might not be the right time to review your new connections, as you have your own business to look after. But as you should know by now, this is when most people get it wrong ... they fail to plan the follow-up.

Take action immediately after the event

Don't put those business cards you collected in the drawer. Instead here's your to-do list:

1. **Put calls in the diary.** This is the very first action to take. When you have agreed – in fact, promised – to call a prospect (in this case Emma), put it in your diary as if it's an appointment with an existing client. Don't forget to record all their contact numbers, highlighting the one they agreed you should use.

2. **Send a note or email**. If the contact date is longer than five working days away, send a note or email saying how much you enjoyed meeting the person and, as promised, you will call them on the agreed date. In this case, as it is only three working days, you won't need to call. You need to decide the best time for the first contact for each separate occasion.

3. **Secure the card information**. Losing the card will mean you lose all the information you have gained. Either enter all the details into your database or staple the card to a blank sheet of paper ready to make the call. If you know the name of the prospect's receptionist or secretary, make a record of that too.

4. **Remember the facts**. Annotate all the cards of the people you met with all relevant information: where you met, when, what type of event it was, any physical features you think may be useful to help you remember them next time you meet. Make a note of any useful piece of small talk to use as a bridge to the next step.

5. **Note the words they used**. What gave you the sign that there might be an opportunity? Making a note of this will help one day in the future. The 'ahaa' moment hits you generally from just one sentence – what was it?

6. **Remember the gatekeeper**. Most people have a pessimistic view of talking to gatekeepers, but change your thinking.

When you treat the gatekeepers with respect and courtesy they often revert from gatekeepers to gate-openers. Many of them are influential people, so treat them properly. It's important that you start building ties with this key person in the chain.

"Many gatekeepers are influential people, so treat them properly."

You're not just networking with your new connection, but also with their connections, which includes the company receptionist and secretary. It's a critical part of the process, particularly when the prospect is hard to contact.

PS

1. Take *immediate action*.

2. Talk is cheap and most people say, 'I'll call', 'I'll email', 'Let's keep in touch', 'I'll introduce you to ...'. If you have said you will do any of these – do them within 24 hours (unless you have agreed otherwise).

3. Speed stuns. What a great way to start a business relationship with your prompt attention.

Chapter

13

Reconnecting by phone

The following Wednesday.

B: *What's on today? Just two internal meetings, no business lunch and off early to play golf. Good. Nice quiet day.*

W: *Good morning Brian. Can I ask you to look a little closer at your diary?*

Once the event is over and you're back to work, it's easy to lose the impetus to keep up with your new connections. But if you've made an appointment to call someone, it's really important you follow through. Relationship building, early on in the process, is all about showing you are reliable and trustworthy.

Don't rely on the idea that they'll remember you, thinking that if they want to get in touch they will. You're the one that spotted the 'ahaa' moment, you're looking for new opportunities and clients, so it's your business to ensure it happens. If you don't follow up, you risk being a networking criminal and are guilty of the crime of time wasting.

This is the seventh stage of the networking pipeline: making calls.

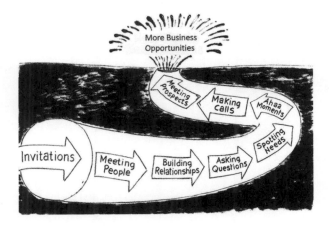

It's your time to grasp the opportunities you've spotted and make the most of those 'ahaa' moments. Making the call cements the relationship and gives you the chance to find out if there's potential for you both to do business together.

> **Top tip**
>
> Avoid committing a networking crime by making sure you follow up.

The usual excuses for failing to follow up include:

- They won't remember me.
- I'm too busy.
- I don't want to appear pushy.
- I've lost their contact details.
- I'm frightened of the gatekeeper.

Remember, you're an expert in your field and they need your help, or you have seen the chance of a possible partnership or collaboration. Adopt a more positive mental attitude. You're following up to share your knowledge and explore possibilities to develop their business, not to sell to reach your targets.

"Remember, you're an expert in your field and they need your help."

If your new connection is waiting for your call and you don't make it, there are serious consequences. It's likely they'll think you're not trustworthy, that you're unreliable and that you don't keep your promises.

There's also the potential damage to the reputation of your organisation. Every time they see the company logo or hear it mentioned, they will think, 'There's an organisation that isn't worth dealing with. I met a really nice guy from there. He promised to call but let me down at the first hurdle.'

I will go further. I believe not following up is worse than going networking in the first place. In the case of Emma, she may have never heard of your company before, but now she has and every time it'll be a negative reminder. She could mention it to others. What's more, are you prepared to waste all that time you invested last week? Oh, and finally, what happens if you meet her again soon? Your credibility is lost and, bearing in mind you are part of a bigger organisation, so too is the credibility of the organisation. It's sad to say the world of business is a desert of unreliability. When you do things when you say you'll do it, you are rare ... an oasis in that desert. So beware of not calling – not only is it likely the relationship will falter, but also other people will lose faith in you, and perhaps your company.

Before the call

Before you make the call, remember the three key steps when building relationships:

- knowing
- liking
- trusting.

You got to know the client at the networking event, so step 1 is ticked off. And you got on well so you might be on your way to ticking step 2 off as well, but if you don't make the call there will be no trust from the start.

As you're looking at that phone, you're imagining all the negatives and feeling nervous.

Just think, you promised to call, Emma has agreed to take your call and she is expecting your call. Furthermore, do you genuinely believe you can help her? If the answer is 'yes', then you must call.

Here are some other ways to reaffirm that initial connection with a new prospect:

- Did they show any doubts about their current suppliers?
- Did you get on well at the event?
- Did they agree to you getting in touch again?

Making the call is simply continuing the conversation you had when you first met. And whilst you don't like hearing 'no', 'no' is the second best answer after 'yes'. One of the worst things in our lives is uncertainty – not knowing what's going to happen. When you make the call and they say 'no,' that's it. You know where you stand. What is the worst that's going to happen?

You are simply phoning to arrange a meeting, if it is relevant, to see if and how you may be able to help. You are not going to start the selling process. If they say 'no' to the meeting, then that's OK. And that's the worst that can happen – they say 'no'. So shrug and move on!

Preparing for the call

As with every success in life, it's all in the planning. So let's start by making time to properly plan this phone call. Give yourself 30 minutes. It might seem a lot, but don't worry – you might only need two minutes but at least there's more time if you need it.

You just don't know where the conversation will go, so it's best to be prepared for every eventuality. Now you've created physical space and time space … that's a good start.

"As with every success in life, it's all in the planning."

Have a look at Emma's business card – or wherever you wrote the notes after you met. Reacquaint yourself with the information – her job title, the company, etc.

Now, what do you know about the company? Always have a look on the internet to see if you can find out any extra information. You might find out how big the company is, if they've won any awards, what sort of press they've had, and any kind of activities they're linked with, such as sponsorship.

If there's something you spot – say that they sponsor the local rugby team and you're a fan – that's going to make the meeting easier. You can't arrive and start talking business immediately. Even then the small talk is key to the building of relationships. But for the phone call, taking the rugby team again, you could check their latest score, which will be more relevant small talk.

Next, get your diary ready to check you can make that meeting. And if you're going to take someone else with you to the meeting, it's also worth having access to their diary too.

Be prepared for their questions

Now, how about preparing answers for some of the questions, she's bound to ask? How do you reply if Emma says, 'Why should we do business with your firm?' Try not to be the same as everyone else, spouting the usual sales pitch:

> We are the best in town; been going for over 30 years; give a really personal service; and we are experts in the field you require. And, of course we are reliable; well, most of the time.

This is just the same as everyone else, and doesn't actually differentiate you at all. Being in existence for 30 years is, please excuse me, an irrelevance. People don't care about your past; they only care about their future and how you can add value to it.

Instead say something like:

> We got on really well the other evening, Emma, and I believe I and my team can help you achieve what you're aiming to do.

When you dial that number, there are four main scenarios that could occur:

Scenario 1

No one answers, it's engaged or you keeping trying the fax number because you're so nervous. Keep trying. If you don't get through on the day you promised, send an email to Emma saying you tried. It doesn't matter desperately if you don't get through. What is most important is that she knows you tried.

If you get no response, you should plan which day are you going to try again. You need to have that ready for the email so she knows when to expect it next. Don't worry if it doesn't suit her, because she'll probably let you know when is better if she replies to your email.

Scenario 2

You might get her voicemail. Say your name slowly and clearly. When you're nervous, people tend to blur their name and the listener may not hear it. You want Emma to hear someone who is confident and upbeat, not someone who is nervous and hesitant. After all, she may be placing her future in your hands. Remind her where you met and that you promised to call today. Say you will call again on either Friday or next Monday.

You may also wish to say, 'Emma, as an alternative, I'll leave you my direct dial'. Are you prepared also to leave your mobile? The easier it is for Emma or any other prospect to contact you, the better. Do ensure you leave your number s-l-o-w-l-y; you know how irritating it is when people leave you a number and you have to replay the message three times to decipher it.

Scenario 3

You might speak to the receptionist or the secretary, and this is probably the reason why most people don't make the call. But think about your gatekeepers – whether an assistant, receptionist or secretary. If I were to ask you about them, I bet you'd say they were very nice people, friendly and always ready to help. After all, they are often the first contacts when people call, so they represent the first impressions of the company.

The reason these people have developed this reputation for behaving like club bouncers is often because of the way they are treated. Aggressive behaviour creates a defensive wall, hence the 'gatekeeper'. All you have you do is treat these people with respect and courtesy and you end up getting help with your goal of speaking to Emma … or her equivalent.

Here's what you might happen if you call. These days you often hear:

> Good morning, Preston Printing Company, Avril speaking, how can I help you?

There is only one word I'd like you to focus on: Avril. I want this dialogue to become familiar now:

> **B:** Good morning, Avril, please may I speak to Emma?
>
> **A:** Who is it please?
>
> **B:** It's Brian Camberton from the Professional Services Company.
>
> **A:** Can you tell me what it's regarding?
>
> **B:** Yes, I met Emma last week at the Premier Networking event. We were in the middle of a conversation – I promised to call her today and she is expecting my call.

So there is your script for the gatekeeper. Two things can happen. First of all, she puts you through. However, maybe Emma's on the phone, not in, or in a meeting. If that's the case, she will ask if she can take a message, put you through to Emma's secretary Mary or her voicemail.

If Emma is unavailable and you are offered all three alternatives, I like the idea of starting to build a relationship with the PA or secretary. My second choice is leaving a message on her voicemail. Finally, ask if you can leave a message with Avril herself.

When you are talking to a busy switchboard operator you're not going to build rapport, and, in a bigger company, the chances of your prospect having a close relationship with the 'front desk' is small. Whoever you leave the message with, the message should be to say you called and that you'll call again.

This is where you can slip up, so have a pre-arranged time when you're going to call again. And don't give up.

If you feel the PA or the receptionist is amenable, ask, 'Please can you help me? If you were me, when do you think the best time would be to call back?' The PA is more likely to know the answer rather than a receptionist at a busy switchboard.

So, we've covered not getting through, getting voicemail and the gatekeeper. What's next? The getting through to Emma.

Scenario 4

You actually get through to Emma.

What to say ... the scripts

If you're nervous or you don't know the other person very well, a phone call can be difficult. You may try to say too much at once, you may speak over one another ... but keep calm and it will be fine.

Try to remember something you learnt from the event

Did they mention they were going away? Ask how the trip went. The fact that you remembered that will impress them.

Don't ask if it's a good time

If you are calling a mobile, the advice here is different. But in all likelihood, Emma will not be sitting there waiting for you to call. She will have things to do and asking her a question like that gives her an option to rush you. You might want to thank her for taking the call if you are put through the screening process. However, if you sense that she's swamped, suggest that you call again. If she is genuinely busy, it's not a good time to have this first conversation. So aim to get permission to call her on a day that is acceptable to her.

Remember the 'ahaa' moment

It's vital that you reintroduce this at this stage of the follow-up. After you do the small talk, rather than just launch straight into, 'I'd like to arrange a meeting,' consider saying the following: 'Remember last week you said you were thinking of buying a company and your present advisors weren't used to handling such matters?' She will hopefully say, 'Yes', to which you can answer, 'I was calling to see if we can arrange a get-together for me to find out more about your company and see how I and my company can perhaps help'. Don't think sell, think help. All you want is to meet, explore ideas and see if you can move the relationship to the next phase.

"Don't think sell, think help."

This ensures that you get to business quickly – you noticed the 'ahaa' moment and now you're doing your best to help. It also means if it's a 'no' you won't be wasting each other's time because you're both on the same page.

Here's my pipeline again:

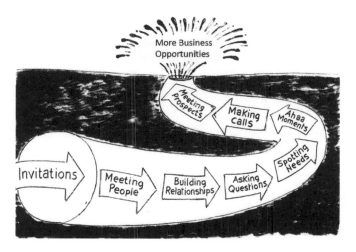

It's this call that leads to the meeting. At the meeting you do the business. But first you need to make the call.

The possible responses

So you phone up and ask for a meeting. There are basically five likely responses to your suggestion.

The first one is she says, 'Yes, let's meet'. However, things don't always go as we'd wish. So let me arm you ready for the other four replies you're going to get.

The second possible response is, 'Can you send me some information first before we meet?' You will need to spend a few moments here to ascertain what information is required. Don't ask her what information she wants, she won't know. Just ask questions about her particular issue, take notes, then agree to send her something. Imagine you are actually at a face-to-face meeting and ask similar questions in the phone call. *Ask permission* to call back in about ten days. Ensure your email or letter refers primarily to her issues and how you believe you can help. Don't talk about yourself, how big your company is and how brilliant you are – she is not interested. All she wants to know is what's in it for her.

Give away free and valuable advice, with a number of options. You will write something like, 'There are three or four ways of dealing with this' and then list them. I repeat, don't be afraid to give advice away free. You are fishing here for a big catch ... it needs some big bait! Explain that at a meeting you can explore each one more fully and offer advice when you sit together. Ensure you mention the fact that you have agreed to call her on a specific day at the end of your email or letter. You might think they are fobbing you off, but until you send information and follow up, you'll never know.

"Give away free and valuable advice."

The third scenario might go like this: 'It's not actually me you need; Joanne deals with that sort of thing.' In this situation, say to Emma, 'If you were me, Emma, how would you move forward from here? Perhaps we could have a three-way meeting for you to introduce me to Joanne and we could take it from there?' At that point you'd know whether she is serious about moving the relationship forward or not. By the way, if this situation ever arises and they say, 'It's so-and-so who deals with that' and you haven't heard of that person, ensure you find out what role that person holds.

The fourth possible response is: 'On reflection, I don't think what you have to offer is for us at the moment.' Don't take this as rejection – if you got on well at the event, and she was happy to take your call, it's not personal. She has rejected the offer of your services, not you personally. Failure? No. It would have been a failure, if you hadn't made the call. Therefore establish if that means 'no now' or 'no never'. If you have built rapport when you meet, people rarely say 'no never'. If that is the case, ask if you can keep in touch and, depending on the response, suggest you contact them again 'later in the year' or 'in the spring'. If you don't get your meeting, ensure you invite Emma to some event.

The fifth possible response is that they want to chat it through there and then. It's unlikely this will happen, but you should be prepared in case it happens. Don't get nervous and end the phone call – compose yourself and start to ask questions as if you're in an actual meeting. If you're giving advice, explain that it's free and with no obligation. Often they'll be grateful for this. But if you are speaking on the phone, don't forget to arrange an actual meeting to discuss more details.

PS

1. If you don't make the call your reputation could be damaged forever.

2. Remember, everyone has fears but the worst that can happen is that the prospect will say, 'No thank you, I have decided not to move forward'.

3. The vast majority of people admit they never make the call. If you pick up the phone, the chances of more business opportunities must be far greater than the average.

Chapter

14

Using LinkedIn to create more business and career opportunities

LinkedIn started out as a job website and even today more than a third of its income comes from HR departments and recruitment agencies using its various premium functions for placing the right people in the right job.

> **B:** *Will, you tell me to go networking and now you want me to spend time doing this social media stuff too. When do I get to see the family and sleep?*

> **W:** *Yes Brian I could sympathise ... but won't! Think of all the hours you spend attending events that really aren't productive. I'm talking about the travel time and the time you spend catching up with personal friends about the local gossip. All I ask you to consider is a way to find, shall we say, two hours a week, maybe whilst you're having a coffee or lunch, to look at LinkedIn.*

The etiquette when using LinkedIn

Everyone knows how to behave at business events, but I am often surprised how that same standard of behaviour is not always prevalent when people network using LinkedIn.

Here are some suggestions:

- Whenever you invite someone to become your level 1 connection, always, I repeat *always*, send them a personal invitation, never the default message LinkedIn itself gives you.

- When someone invites you to connect, and you view their profile, find it interesting, but can't remember who they are, send them a message asking why they want to connect, including an apology that in fact you may have met previously.

- When someone accepts your invitation, always send a message back thanking them and offer to introduce them to your other contacts if the situation is right.

- When you accept an invitation, again thank them, then offer to broker introductions if you can.

- If you are in the advice-giving business, consider giving away free advice when you connect. I have hyperlinked articles about helping people enhance their knowledge of LinkedIn. I live by the mantra, 'The more you tell, the more you sell'!

Your next job

Ensure your profile is up to date and reflects your knowledge, experience and expertise. Put yourself in the global shop window; you never know who is seeking you out.

Avoid cold-calling to meet new prospects

Does this conversation between you (Y) and your client Jo (J) resonate?

J: Thanks so much for what you have done for me.

Y: That's very kind of you. Please don't forget to mention me to others who you think have got the same issues.

J: Oh don't you worry, I won't forget; I really am grateful.

And off Jo goes, full of good intentions and bonhomie. But what happens next?

She gets in her car or back to her office; back to the phone calls, emails and everyday issues we all have. Before the day is out, she has forgotten you. Not intentionally; it's just you're now not too high up on her to-do list.

Drum roll

This is where Linkedin can be invaluable. When you have asked them to introduce you to 'others' it really is rather pointless. It's like saying to someone, 'We must get together soon!' Nothing definite, nothing focused.

Ten action points

1. Invite Jo to connect on LinkedIn.
2. If she does, you are now level 1 contacts and you have one particular and valuable benefit. What is it?
3. Unless Jo hides her contacts, you now have access to her level 1 contacts (i.e. your level 2 contacts). It's her 'little black book'.
4. Start looking through her connections to find someone you think might be worth starting a business relationship with.
5. Do as much research on this 'target' before moving forward to ensure it could be the right fit for you and your firm. You don't want to waste Jo's time – or your own for that matter.
6. When you find that person, let's call him Ben, ask Jo to broker a warm introduction for you. You will then know how really happy Jo has been!
7. Do not use the 'introduction' button on LinkedIn. Phone or email Jo to find out how well she knows Ben. After all, there are literally millions of people linked who have never met. If Jo is happy to make the introduction, work out the best way for her to introduce you to Ben.
8. Subtly ensure Jo says nice things about you to Ben!
9. The best way to move the relationship forward is to suggest a three-way get-together. Keep it informal; it's best to meet off work space and spend most of the time on small talk. It's the start of a relationship. Spend 80 per cent of your time being interested by asking probing and clarifying questions. Don't try to sell your firm.

> **10.** Once you feel you are building some rapport with Ben
> ... you're on your own. It's now down to you to do the
> business! But not at that first meeting.

Other proactive activities using LinkedIn

Construct a targeted prospect list. Use advanced features like tags, network sorting options, and LinkedIn contacts to group prospects who have similar buyer characteristics. Download your connections database to an Excel or similar database. You can then filter and sort the names for use outside LinkedIn. Consider upgrading to one of the premium LinkedIn accounts to receive additional profile sorting and saving options.

Start to link in with present and past friends, work colleagues and university mates, etc. My advice is to only link with people you know. The more contacts you have at level 1, the more level 2 contacts you have. Until LinkedIn came along, you never knew who your contacts had in their network; but you do now, so make the best use of your network.

There are two key groups of importance in your business life. People with whom you have a relationship already and people you'd like to build a relationship with from scratch. The second group can be approached 'cold' but why would you do this if someone you know and with whom you have a good relationship can make the introduction?

"If you think LinkedIn important, set aside time each week to work on it."

Link in with others in your company to ensure cross-selling occurs more and your profile is raised internally. If you think LinkedIn important, set aside time each week to work on it.

Maybe two sessions of 45 minutes? Join groups relevant to your career and job. Contribute your knowledge and expertise with advice questions and articles in those groups. Comment on other peoples' views.

On a weekly basis, update the status box shown on your home page with relevant business news and advice. You can always hyperlink other peoples' articles. Learn how to use the advanced search function so you seek out key decision makers and potential clients.

PS

1. Social networking will *never* take the place of attending events. If you have limited time, always choose to meet people face-to-face.

2. There should be no need to cold call prospects. Ask the people you know to introduce you to people they know.

3. Behave as graciously online as you would when you attend networking events.

Chapter

15

Meeting again

Now for the eighth and final stage of the networking pipeline – meetings.

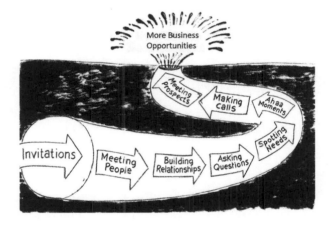

This is everything you've been working towards: you accepted the invitation, you met some nice people, you found some potentially interesting opportunities and now you're having a meeting to talk it through.

Those worries you had about the networking event being a waste of time were unfounded, and this meeting could lead to even more opportunities for you and your organisation. Time to congratulate yourself!

Be prepared

Now you've got the meeting in the bag, it's important you plan and prepare properly. Just like before going into the event, and before making the phone call, it's imperative you prepare.

- When and where are you meeting?
- Who is going with you?
- Are you taking material with you?
- What do you want to achieve?

But before you start crafting an all-singing, all-dancing PowerPoint presentation with a history of your company, some pictures of the offices, and details of similar deals you've done – stop. Avoid the classic mistake of focusing on you and your company.

Remember, initially, your client doesn't care about your company's past, who works there, its offices and the technical stuff. All they want to know is how you can help them, and the only way you can do that is to be prepared to ask intelligent questions and to answer any questions they are going to ask. There will be time to explain your knowledge and experience later … and even then it is wise to keep it brief.

"Be prepared to ask intelligent questions and to answer any questions."

Going back to your meeting with Emma, you've already done lots of research before the call, so reacquaint yourself and Aimee, your assistant, with Emma's situation. Simply ask relevant questions, take notes, listen attentively and make some proposals. People don't want to be sold to; you hate the process, so don't do it. You did your selling last week at the event.

Here's a better way to go about it. When you and Aimee get to their premises, be alert from the moment you arrive. You may pick up some useful information by just observing, which again shows you're genuinely interested. It's likely you'll be kept waiting for a few moments.

Ensure you glance around the reception. There may be award plaques on the wall or pictures of some of their products. Any last-minute information you gather can only be useful.

In the meeting

Once you're in the meeting and everyone has shaken hands, no doubt tea or coffee will be served. A little small talk will be good. It might involve something you've just seen or maybe something in the office. Family photos, certificates, even sports trophies are always simple topics to mention.

If you're struggling for topics, go back to the networking event. How about, 'It was a really good event the other evening, wasn't it, Emma?' You shouldn't just launch into, 'Right, let's get down to business' within two minutes of arriving. Avoid repeating yourself though, so don't go harping on about her last holiday if you've already spoken about it.

Having been through the pleasantries, they will expect you to start selling. Don't. Remember the 'ahaa' moment – what was it she said? Use it in your introduction. How about something like: 'Thank you both for seeing us. Last week, Emma, you said …'– and here insert what she did say that prompted your 'ahaa' moment. 'So, tell us more about the company, what exactly you would like to happen and let's see how we can help you.'

It's really that simple. Give your client full command over radio station WII FM (what's in it for me?) The spotlight has to be on her and the business. You and Aimee are just the side show. Your thinking has to have a modern approach … WIIFY (what's in it for you?).

Top tip

Don't sell, let them buy!

As you proceed through the meeting, ask yourself:

- Is there a real problem that needs a solution?
- Is something required and are they unable to find a solution by themselves?
- Is there a commitment to change things and move forward?

- Are they in a position where they are finally ready to take action?

- Are they willing to invest in a solution?

- Have they the time, inclination and money to do what it takes to make the change?

- Can they picture the future and imagine the outcome they are aiming to achieve?

If you get positive signs on all of the above and you believe you and your organisation as a whole can help them, then you can go into the presentation of your services. You want to assure them that you can help to solve their problem and produce the results they want. But don't dwell on this part.

You don't need to do a hard sell. Your word-of-mouth marketing largely got the job done last week at the event. Of course, briefly explain how you'd approach their situation and perhaps provide a few examples of past success, such as testimonials. But keep it brief and relevant to Emma and her company.

Put in plain words as briefly as possible what you can offer, how the process would work, and what is likely to happen. Also explain the kind of results to expect. Don't be afraid to ask if they have any questions – this is vital to ensure they understand what you're discussing and to check any reservations. In fact ask, 'Who's got the first question?'

"Put in plain words as briefly as possible what you can offer."

If you're discussing money or terms, name them and see what they say. If there's a silence, don't be tempted to break it. They could just be thinking.

The actions of effective and confident networkers

So you see, networking doesn't have to be scary. At first, as with any new activity, it may take a while to feel 100 per cent comfortable doing it, but as long as you follow the process I have shown you and approach networking with a new, positive mindset, it's amazing how quickly you will notice the changes. I heard this recently and it's relevant to anything new we face in life:

Do the things that you fear and the fear will disappear.

Always bear in mind the following. Confident and effective networkers:

- are awake, alive and alert, and recognise opportunities everywhere;
- see all new contacts as potential business prospects;
- have a giving mentality;
- make the first move when meeting new people;
- have an interesting opening statement, explaining how they help their clients;
- understand the power of remembering names;
- are good listeners – and let the other person do most of the talking;
- know that small talk is the most important talk;
- ask for other people's business cards;
- follow up and are persistent without pestering.

PS

1. Think mutual benefits and show genuine interest in your new contact.

2. Less can often be more when you're pitching.

3. The more the prospect talks and asks questions, the more you should realise they are interested.

Chapter

16

Maintaining relationships

During these challenging times, people are so busy that once the meeting, call or transaction is finished they're off to something else and you will, more often than not, be forgotten. When they do decide to do new or more business with you, you want to be their first choice. Therefore, it's important your prospects remain aware of you, and current clients and customers come back for more.

There's more to business than just a transaction. Building a relationship helps you establish a bond. Some clients are even willing to pay more for a product and/or service if they have a personal connection with you, who represents your company: people 'buy people' before they buy the product or service.

"Building a relationship helps you establish a bond."

Following up and maintaining relationships starts with a dilemma.

Those cross-roads may be familiar – we came across them when we discussed making a follow-up call after having met someone at an event. But let me reiterate: you are following up to see how your expertise and knowledge might add value to your prospect's/existing client's business. When you think of business development being about helping other businesses, the follow-up and keeping in touch aspect of relationship building should allay any fears you may have taking the left path. Here are various suggestions to maintain those relationships.

Keep in touch

If clients and customers recently placed an order or you provided a service, ask them for feedback. Showing you care about what they think speaks volumes about your commitment to them. On some occasions the comments won't always be great; you need this feedback to ensure you get it right next time. When you put it right and give them some valuable extras by way of an apology, it can often strengthen the relationship.

If they have not done business with you in a while, remind them you're still there and available to help. Every so often I send a quick note to say something to the effect of:

> Hope all is well with you.
>
> Let me remind you of how I am still helping clients ... it's very quick.
>
> I show people how to enhance their face-to-face networking skills and how to profit from the use of LinkedIn.
>
> My advice is for anyone who attends business events in any capacity they may hold, or who needs to get real value when using LinkedIn.

I then send a couple of relevant articles I have written with their logo on, showing our relationship isn't all about the sell.

Pick up the phone

This seems to be going out of fashion, but if most of your communication takes place via email, it's still so important to pick up the phone occasionally to touch base. Personal interaction is still critical in this 'virtual' world.

Branch out

You may have a particular target market in mind, but to reach it doesn't mean that you network with just that group. Find groups that don't mirror your target market and build relationships with their members. That is the benefit of networking. People you meet know people who might be future clients.

Become a resource

'Give without remembering; receive without forgetting' (Elizabeth Bibesco) resonates soundly for me. Always look for opportunities to support someone, even if they don't always mean you'll get an immediate return on your efforts. Broker introductions, help with an event or offer suggestions. When that person, or someone they know, are looking for a product or service that you offer, you're more likely to be foremost in their mind. The more you get to know them, the more you'll be able to offer assistance by knowing their needs.

"Always look for opportunities to support someone."

Networking has been around since time immemorial, but it was only in the late twentieth century the word came into vogue. In 1985 in California Dr Ivan Misner set up BNI (Business Network International), a marketing referral business. The whole objective is for members, who meet weekly for breakfast, to refer business to each other. Their tag line is 'Givers gain', meaning the more referrals you give, in the long run, the more you should gain. Great theory, but one that in the real world doesn't always work. However, it worked for me – having been a member for a few years, a fellow member helped me move from accountancy to what I do now.

Write a note

Adding the personal touch of a hand-written thank you note shows clients you appreciate them for giving you business. There are not enough acknowledgements today, I find. I know for me it is vital I thank anyone who gives me advice, introduces me to new business or writes to me saying how much they enjoyed my training or presentation.

Tailor your approach

Your customers vary in workload, style of communication and desire to share information, so your approach should be just as diverse. If your customer doesn't appreciate you just stopping by, then call in advance to set up a time, or invite them out for coffee.

Your approach needs to be genuine and within your comfort zone or it may backfire on you. If you aren't comfortable with face-to-face interactions, pick up the phone or just send an email.

Speed stuns

When you get an enquiry after an event or you have promised to action something, do it very quickly; put it at the top of your to-do list. It shows your commitment to the relationship and shows what a reliable and trustworthy person you are, and so builds confidence in you and your company. Also, if an issue arises, take action and make it your priority to resolve it imme-diately. Sometimes errors and how we resolve them provide an exceptional opportunity to show our commitment to the cus-tomer – take a bad situation and make it a positive.

Listen, listen, listen

Your customer may provide clues that might be your portal to providing a personal touch. If they indicate that their child is heading off to their first year of university, or they are taking a long-awaited holiday, jot these things down on a calendar so you can ask how things went when you do a follow-up call. Or they might state that it was their birthday last week. Put that on your calendar so the following year you can send a birthday greeting. Lots of the social networks, such as Facebook, LinkedIn and Plaxo, will prompt you when it is a fellow member's birthday.

Building any type of a relationship takes time, whether it's a personal or business relationship. It's an essential part of your business to help maintain and grow your customer base. As part of your daily to-do list, make a point to connect with one client every day. You may be surprised at the impact.

"Building any type of a relationship takes time, whether it's a personal or business relationship."

PS

1. Follow up quickly when you spot an opportunity.
2. Grade clients according to their importance to you. They are all important, but some are more important than others. For 'grade A' clients ensure you contact them at least quarterly if you haven't had contact otherwise.
3. Be reliable. Do what you say you're going to do and do it when you say you're going to do it.

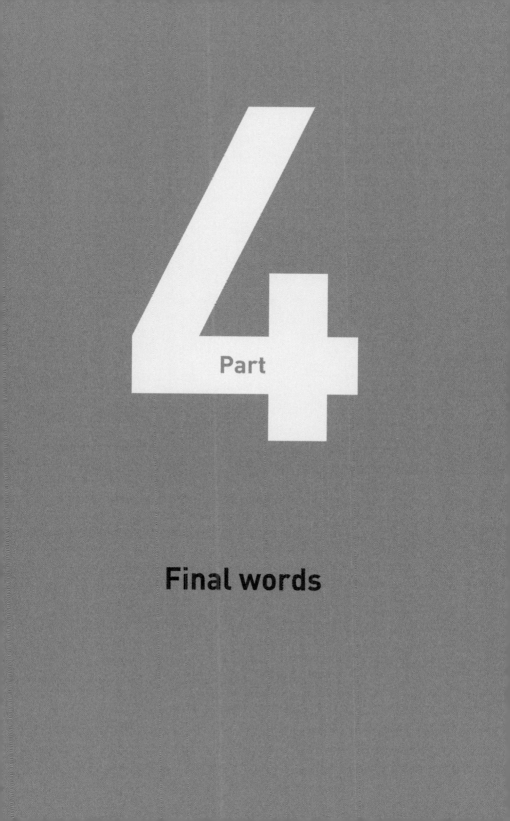

Part

4

Final words

Chapter 17

Why networking matters

Are you an all-round modern-day professional or technical expert? You are when:

- you know your subject matter intimately;
- you understand what others and your clients are trying to achieve;
- you want to provide your clients with advice or products to ensure they are ahead of their opposition;
- you show genuine interest by asking effective questions and listening empathetically;
- you want to build a long-term relationship and don't just sell services to meet your own goals;
- you realise that all the IT and web technology will never replace the important face-to-face contact;
- you understand that your relationship is about *creating* value for your client, not just paying lip service to it;
- you do what you say you're going to do, and you do it *when* you say you're going to do it.

That's a good start, but in today's competitive climate it's equally important that:

- you help bring in business opportunities of your own;
- you offer services to clients and prospects, which perhaps they didn't know about;
- you introduce clients to colleagues or other professionals, outside your sphere of expertise, who can offer additional advice and support.

In short, today, you need to contribute to the area of business development. This can be directly or indirectly, depending on your role. After all, you should be proud of the organisation you represent and want it to succeed.

"You need to contribute to the area of business development."

You are undoubtedly an expert and authority in your chosen topic and as a consequence feel safe, secure and comfortable in providing technical advice. You are in control and feel protected by your knowledge. But when it comes to leaving the office and going out to attract more business, do you feel equally au fait and safe?

Your future in their hands?

Even today, most of your new business comes from recommendations, referrals and existing clients coming back for more. This means you have a good name and provide a good service. That's great news. But what it also means is that others control the speed of growth of your client and fee base and other types of business opportunities. If you are satisfied with this, then there's no need to make changes.

However, if that is not the case, you need to follow the advice in this book so that you can become more proactive in seeking new business opportunities, whilst still remaining within your comfort zone. It will require a great shift in your thinking, but what you actually do will alter very little. Yet it will be those little differences that will revolutionise your approach to and your successes with business development.

Change your thinking

There are many people who consider selling and marketing as essentially dishonest and manipulative. If that's how you think, the chances are you will resist change. This resistance is expressed in sentiments such as:

- I just don't do selling and marketing – that's someone else's job.
- I feel uncomfortable talking about myself and blowing my own trumpet.
- I sound phoney when I talk about the benefits I offer.
- I'm just not the marketing type.
- I can't sell myself.

It's no wonder many professionals and technicians struggle with marketing and feel uncomfortable when talking to prospective clients about their services. Business development becomes a 'necessary evil'. The best way to get past these quite understandable feelings is to look at business development and the marketing of your services from a new perspective.

The most important change to make is to begin to think in terms of 'helping create value so both parties benefit' as opposed to 'selling'. If you have knowledge in an area useful to your client or prospective client, tell yourself, 'I can add value to this person's business or personal circumstances'. That way, you won't feel like you are imposing, but quite the opposite. Unless you are in the fraud and rip-off business, the value of your advice will, most probably, far outweigh the fee you charge. If not, dare I suggest you are in the wrong job! When you are looking for alliances, joint ventures and partnerships, everyone wins.

Networking and business development

Networking is one of the most important facets of business development. Naturally, the more people you meet and the more relationships you build, the more likely you are to create more business opportunities. But do not think of networking as a means to subtly manipulate the people you meet, coaxing them into buying your services through shameless boasting about the quality of your company.

"The more relationships you build, the more likely you are to create more business opportunities."

The essence of networking is the building of relationships. As we saw in Chapter 13, three fundamental steps need to take place:

- getting to know people
- getting them to like you (and you them)
- getting them to trust you (and you them).

The first two steps can take no time at all. We all know about first impressions, which, although not always accurate, tend to become long lasting. The trust takes much longer to build; we have to earn trust and that can only be done through the investment of time and by keeping in touch.

There is little argument that 'people buy people' before they buy services and products. In fact, I believe we all buy the person first, the service they have to offer second and the company itself last. When you are out networking, don't think about selling your company, its services or its products. Simply sell yourself. When you do this well, you are the gateway through which business will come, whatever role or expertise you have. When you make a great impression and someone has a need for the type of services your company offers, you become the initial point of contact. In fact, all of a sudden you are head of business development at that juncture! We go to networking events simply to create the platform to start or re-establish relationships, that's all. Once the relationship is in place, it's amazing how quickly the business opportunities grow.

"When you are out networking, don't think about selling your company. Simply sell yourself."

But I hate networking!

Let's leave the word networking now; it conjures up too many negative images. Let's talk about attending business-related events. These manifest themselves in many different formats. They can include:

- dinners – small or large
- conferences
- seminars
- exhibitions
- corporate hospitality – as either guest or host
- one-to-one lunches with an existing client or contact
- cocktail receptions
- sporting or cultural events
- social events of any nature with clients or business connections
- even formal networking clubs!

If where you go relates to 'work', in some form or another, then you are potentially networking, i.e. building or reinforcing relationships. Natural networkers do it any time, any place, anywhere. Even at parties and weddings, people (mainly men) talk business quite early on in a conversation. In fact, some men only have two topics of conversation … business and sport.

Socialising, partying and networking

Most people like socialising and partying, but struggle with the third, networking. However, all three types of events are virtually the same. At each, we meet people – some we know and some we don't. We eat, we drink, we converse, we laugh, we start or continue to build relationships, we talk, we listen, and we have general social interaction. You can have fun, pleasure and excitement at all three, so is there a difference? Yes, one important difference being the amount of alcohol you drink. Representing yourself and/or your organisation at a business-related event and getting intoxicated is unlikely to be good for business! However, the most important difference is that at a business-related event, you should be actively seeking your 'ahaa' moment.

What is an 'ahaa' moment?

The fundamental reason we go to business-related events is to spot the 'ahaa' moment; that moment when we hook on to a new piece of information, which we believe could be beneficial to the development of our business.

The 'ahaa' moment comes when someone says something, prompting you to think:

- Ahaa, I think I can help you with that issue.
- Ahaa, I can introduce you to that person you've been trying to meet.
- Ahaa, that's a useful piece of information about our competitors.
- Ahaa, that's new technical knowledge I wasn't aware of.
- Ahaa, that person isn't happy in their job. We have a vacancy for someone like that.
- Ahaa, that's the sort of new role I'd like.
- Ahaa, they're not happy with their existing advisors.
- Ahaa, we are looking for a new supplier for those services or products.

Remember, it could also be an existing client who says something, prompting you to think, 'Ahaa, there could be more work here' or, even more importantly, 'Ahaa, they're not 100 per cent happy with our services, we'd better correct that'. Ultimately, if you don't spot an 'ahaa' moment of any sort, or worse still, you don't even look for one, going to a business-connected event will really be a waste of your precious personal time. Time you could give to the family, the gym, your hobby or simply time spent relaxing at home.

The numbers game

Networking is ultimately all based on numbers. The more events we go to, the more people we get to know and the more 'ahaa' moments we hear. Many businesses use the phrase 'sales pipeline' in their marketing and business development as a measure of potential new business to be done in the future. The pipeline often starts with an initial meeting with a prospect, moving through a series of sales processes, and ends with a successful (or sometimes unsuccessful) conclusion. In turn, the networking pipeline, described throughout this book, will help to create considerably more of those first meetings.

"If you don't go, you'll never know."

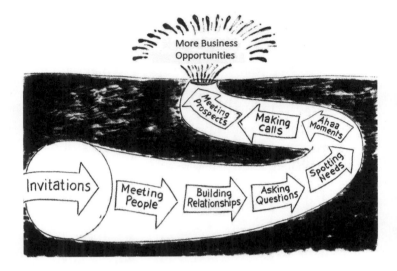

This is the networking pipeline. It finishes with the first meeting, linking nicely to the first step in the sales pipeline. It all starts with the number of business-related invitations you accept. When you decline 19 out of 20, your pipeline will be pretty thin. If you accept 19 out of 20, it's no surprise the opportunities for growing your business increase dramatically. Don't get me wrong, you're not expected to give your whole life to your job but, if you do want more business generated by your own efforts, decline fewer invitations than you do at present.

The heart of this book deals with the 'Networking Life of Brian', charting his growth into a master networker. But as Brian will testify, the first lesson to learn about networking is this:

If you don't go, you'll never know.

PS

1. Networking is just communicating, so there should be nothing to worry about.

2. The large majority of 'strangers' are nice just like you. Remember that when you attend events.

3. You will do better in your job or business when you are an effective and confident networker.

Chapter

18

Understanding how to network with the opposite sex

The big gender networking gap

I can only generalise here, because of course all men and all women are not the same. However, having studied the subject for many years now, I will share my findings.

"Neither gender is better at networking ... just different."

If there is one area of our lives where men and women are different it is when we attend events (i.e. network). We think differently, we behave differently and we talk differently. Neither gender is better at networking ... just different. You will become an even better networker when you understand this and act accordingly.

The key difference

Men often go networking with the idea 'I need to get something from this', whereas women go networking for the purest of reasons – to build relationships. When it comes to small talk and building rapport, men come a very miserable second; women are usually far better at it.

Be sensitive to others

Over the years I have presented to many women whose perception is that men generally prefer to stay on the safe topics of business and sport. Cetainly, my experience is that men who support football teams do like to engage in that topic regularly.

One woman I spoke to became very animated when I mentioned that men were not as good at small talk as women. No, it wasn't the gender issue she had a problem with, it was football! The previous evening she had been to a dinner where there were ten people at the table: two women and eight men. She wasn't sitting near the other woman. 'Do you know what,' she told me, 'for one hour, yes one hour,' by now her voice had risen, 'those eight men talked football, bl**dy football! Even though all my colleagues were senior to me and there were guests at the table, I just couldn't help myself. I asked them if we could possibly change the subject. Even then I felt they could have spent the rest of the night on the same topic.'

In their great book *Why Men Don't Listen and Women Can't Read Maps* (Orion, 1991) Allan and Barbara Pease suggest:

> It's been known for thousands of years men aren't great conversationalists, particularly when compared to women. For women speech continues to have such a clear purpose: to build relationships and make friends. For men, to talk is to relate facts.

Networking is an inclusive sport (oh dear, there we go again), not exclusive. Be sensitive to all the people in your group and consider their feelings and views.

"Be sensitive to all the people in your group and consider their feelings and views."

The primary objective of a man's networking tends to be more business-based and less orientated towards friendship. Women tend to be less obvious when building their networks and rely more on the personal relationship rather than facts and WIIFM (what's in it for me?). I can only generalise, but have seen evidence for my thinking.

Men do often use sport as an instrument for building relationships. Many women find it easier to discuss personal information, families and friends. It's just how it is. Women may be subtler and more observant when networking. One of the greatest tools women have, so-called female intuition, comes into play very quickly when meeting strangers. I can't tell you the number of times my wife Trudie has said, 'Don't trust him', 'Something unusual there', 'I told you she was no good'. And so on. The fact of the matter is she's more often than not correct. This, by the way, is from a woman who gets on with everyone but can just seem to pinpoint the wrong 'uns.

As Allan and Barbara Pease explain:

> A woman uses words to show participation and build relationships and so, for her, words are a form of reward. If she likes you, she is buying what you're saying or wants to be your friend, she'll talk to you a lot. The reverse is true …

The irony for me is that, whilst women might make much better networkers, they refuse far more invitations than men and have less opportunity to actually use their inherent and ingrained skills. Why? Because often, they don't feel as if they are being taken seriously. This reason I have heard is not from younger women, but from more experienced women in senior roles. The advice I give is to ask really good searching questions when talking to men and I then believe you break down those 'gender issues' very quickly.

Many women are skilled at the small talk but often don't (comfortably) move to the business talk. This surely is important; after all, you are there to create a business opportunity. So do move on to the business at the appropriate moment.

The big differences when networking

As well as the differences between men and women in conversation styles, here are some more variations:

- As a general rule when talking to others, women stand facing the person they're talking to; men stand side-by-side. I believe this is again because woman give their full attention to the person they are with; men keep their options open. If the person they are talking to has no interest in them, the man will be scouring the room looking for his next quarry! It goes back to the start of time when the women were bringing up the children – and networking – and we men were out there alone … hunting!

- Toilets! I often recommend to women attending events where they think they will know no one to go to the toilet as they arrive, even if their hair and make-up doesn't need improvement. Why? Well I have been reliably informed they often get chatting in front of the mirror and they can then make an entrance with their new 'friend'. Even once the event is underway there is often a possibility to strike up a conversation in the toilets.

- Men don't talk to other men in toilets!

- I find it hard to approach a group of three men at an event. Give me a mixed group or three women and I'm fine. But for women, they should always approach groups of two or three men, as long as they are standing in open format (i.e. not closed looking as if they are in a rugby scrum). As long as a woman gives eye contact to each, smiles and asks something like, 'Do you mind if I join you?' she will always, well nearly always, be welcomed in.

- There will be far more instances where a man will approach a single woman at an event rather than the other way round. If you are a woman – don't hold back; that man is praying for someone to come and talk to him. You never know, it could be your next biggest transaction. I believe as long as it is a business event there should be no gender issue here.

- Many men speak in short phrases with little or no details, whereas women often speak in paragraphs, giving lots of story-like details. Men want and need the 'bottom line' first, while women want and need details, details, details. That is not to say that men are not interested in getting the details, because they often do want them, but only after getting the bottom line answer to their question. Women enjoy the suspense of working up to the bottom line, for the joy is in the telling of the story. Men, however, experience this enjoyment as agitation, sometimes becoming very frustrated while waiting for the punch line or bottom line to the story. To effectively communicate with someone of the opposite sex, in your personal or career relationships, you must change your approach.

The differences between men and women go far beyond the obvious. Take, for example, the matter of eye contact. On average, women maintain direct eye contact while speaking for twelve seconds, whereas men maintain eye contact for three seconds. Wow! Ladies, think about the last time you carried on a conversation with your husband or partner. Perhaps you maintained direct eye contact with him for several seconds at a time, before looking down or somewhere else in the room, and then returning to direct eye contact for several more seconds. What if you were to change your approach by only maintaining direct eye contact with him for a couple of brief seconds, perhaps looking away more often so he doesn't feel like he's been placed under a microscope? If you've ever experienced the feeling that comes with being stared at by someone for what seems like a very long time, you can then better understand how your husband or partner feels in these situations.

"The differences between men and women go far beyond the obvious."

Men, think about the last time you were speaking with your wife or partner. How often did you look away, look down at your feet or back at the television or newspaper, while conversing with her? Is it any wonder then that she thinks you aren't listening to her? She may even begin to raise the tone and volume of her voice to make sure you are even hearing her speak to you. What if you were to change your approach by increasing the number of seconds you maintain direct eye contact with her, perhaps giving some verbal signals to signify to her that you really are listening, occasionally leaning in towards her and physically touching her during conversation? She will love it! And she will love *you* even more because she will know you are paying close attention to her every word, and won't feel as though she's being ignored.

There should be no touching at the business event but, men, do consider the previous paragraph when it comes to building rapport with the opposite sex.

Advice to both genders – try something different

Having pointed out what the differences are, let me suggest some new approaches to take when dealing with the opposite sex.

Men

- Expand your topic range with women and don't talk business too quickly.
- Family is a great topic but approach it in a sensitive manner.
- Even if women are standing in closed formats, it doesn't necessarily mean they are having a private conversation. Unless they are very animated, consider approaching them and introducing yourself.
- Don't think approaching a woman on her own is going to be taken the wrong way, as long as you are professional and business-like in your attitude.
- Give your full attention and don't lose interest too quickly. Ask more questions and get into more detail about the subject matter. When the conversation is over, behave in the correct manner (as explained in Chapter 6).
- Treat women with the same respect and courtesy as you do your own gender. Remember you never know who they know, even if you consider the person you're talking to is not very senior. I have had many instances when a trainee professional has gone back to her firm to enthuse about my presentation, leading to an introduction to more senior colleagues. This has led to work for me.
- Approaching mixed-gender groups at a networking event is always a safe option, as there is plenty of choice of conversation topics and a mix of conversation styles.

Women

- The men are there to 'hunt' so if they want to get into business, quickly go with the flow.

- Don't think approaching a man on his own is going to be taken the wrong way, as long as you are professional and business-like in your attitude.

- Consider knowing the bare facts about football! A little knowledge can really impress the football fan.

- Try to fight your natural instincts and stand in open format, unless you specifically don't want anyone approaching.

- The toilets are a good place to start or reinforce relationships. Use them strategically.

- Open-formatted all-male groups will always, well nearly always, be welcoming.

- Your instincts will tell you whether a closed group of women is welcoming or not. I'm a man, so can't give advice here!

- Approaching mixed-gender groups at a networking event is always a safe option, as there is plenty of choice of conversation topics and a mix of conversation styles.

PS

Ensure you understand and accept when networking with the other gender that men and women:

1. Think differently.

2. Talk differently.

3. Act differently.

And when all's been said and done

Personality traits

1. **Be enthusiastic** – about yourself, your work and the company you represent.

2. **Be organised** – plan and prepare before attending events.

3. **Be a nice person** – be friendly, polite, courteous, open and respectful to everyone.

4. **Be generous** – and have a giving spirit. Don't think 'What's in it for me?' but 'What's in it for you?'.

5. **Be reliable to build trust** – do what you say you're going to do when you say you'll do it.

6. **Be persistent** – if you spot an opportunity, don't hear 'no', only 'not yet'.

7. **Be patient** – it takes time to build relations.

8. **Ask the right questions** – when you do this, you'll get better answers and create more business opportunities.

9. **Listen actively** – we learn nothing by talking, only by listening.

10. **Get your timings right** – know when to talk, when to listen, when to move into groups, when to leave, when to follow up and at what intervals.

AND WHEN ALL'S BEEN SAID AND DONE

In summary

- When you next receive a business invitation, will you accept or decline?
- How much planning and preparation will you be doing before attending?
- Which person or which groups of people are you going to approach?
- How are you going to start building relationships and get people to like you?
- What conversations are you going to have and what open questions are you going to be asking?
- How are you going to spot the 'ahaa' moment, leading to potential opportunities?
- Are you always going to pick up the phone after you've spotted this potential opportunity?
- How many more meetings are you going to arrange as a result of the phone call?
- How persistent are you going to be without pestering?
- How much do you want to succeed in your career or make more money?

Index